Annotated Teacher's Edition

. . . a resource of student activities
to accompany
Write Source

Level 6

WRITE SOURCE®

GREAT SOURCE EDUCATION GROUP
a division of Houghton Mifflin Company
Wilmington, Massachusetts

A Few Words About the *Write Source SkillsBook: Level 6*

Before you begin . . .

The *SkillsBook* provides you with opportunities to practice the editing and proofreading skills presented in *Write Source*. That book contains guidelines, examples, and models to help you complete your work in the *SkillsBook*.

Each *SkillsBook* activity includes a brief introduction to the topic and examples illustrating how to complete that activity. You will be directed to the page numbers in the text for additional information and examples. The "Proofreading Activities" focus on punctuation and the mechanics of writing. The "Sentence Activities" provide practice in sentence combining and in correcting common sentence problems. The "Parts of Speech Activities" highlight each of the eight parts of speech.

The **Next Step**

Most activities include a **Next Step** at the end of the exercise. The purpose of the Next Step is to provide ideas for follow-up work that will help you apply what you have learned to your own writing.

Authors: Pat Sebranek and Dave Kemper

Printed in the United States of America

International Standard Book Number: 978-0-669-50710-2 (student edition)

7 8 9 10 - POO - 09 08

ational Standard Book Number: 978-0-669-50713-3 (teacher's edition)

7 8 9 10 - POO - 09 08

Table of Contents

Proofreading Activities

Marking Punctuation

End Punctuation 1 and 2 **3**
Commas Between Items in a Series **7**
Commas to Set Off Nonrestrictive Phrases and Clauses **9**
Commas to Set Off Explanatory Phrases **11**
Commas to Separate Long Introductory Phrases and Clauses **13**
Commas in Compound Sentences **15**
Comma Practice 1, 2, and 3 **17**
Semicolons and Colons **21**
Punctuating Dialogue 1 and 2 **23**
Quotation Marks and Italics **25**
Apostrophes 1, 2, and 3 **27**
Hyphens and Dashes **31**
Punctuation Review 1, 2, and 3 **33**
Mixed Review **39**

Editing for Mechanics

Capitalization 1 and 2 **41**
Capitalization and Abbreviations **45**
Plurals **47**
Numbers **49**

Improving Spelling

Spelling **51**

Using the Right Word

Using the Right Word 1, 2, 3, and 4 **53**
Using the Right Word Review 1 and 2 **58**

Sentence Activities

Sentence Basics

Subjects and Predicates 1 and 2 **63**
Compound Subjects and Predicates **67**
Clauses **69**
Prepositional Phrases **71**
Transitions **73**

Sentence Problems

Sentence Fragments **75**
Run-Ons 1 and 2 **77**
Sentence Problems Review 1 and 2 **81**
Rambling Sentences **84**
Subject-Verb Agreement 1 and 2 **85**
Subject-Verb Agreement Review **89**

Sentence Variety

Combining Sentences Using Key Words **91**
Combining Sentences with a Series of Words or Phrases **93**
Combining Sentences with Compound Subjects and Predicates **95**
Kinds of Sentences 1 and 2 **97**
Types of Sentences **101**
Compound Sentences 1 and 2 **103**
Complex Sentences 1 and 2 **107**
Expanding Sentences **111**
Expanding Sentences with Phrases **113**
Expanding Sentences with Phrases and Clauses **115**
Sentence Variety Review 1 and 2 **117**

Parts of Speech Activities

Nouns

Nouns 123
Singular and Plural Nouns 124
Common and Proper Nouns 125
Concrete and Abstract Nouns 127
Using Nouns 129
Specific Nouns 131

Pronouns

Pronouns 133
Antecedents 134
Indefinite Pronouns 135
Subject and Object Pronouns 137
Possessive Pronouns 139

Verbs

Verbs 1 and 2 141
Helping Verbs 145
Verb Tenses 1 and 2 147
Irregular Verbs 1 and 2 151
Irregular Verb Review 155
Transitive and Linking Verbs 157

Adjectives

Adjectives 159
Special Kinds of Adjectives 161
Forms of Adjectives 163
Colorful Adjectives 1 and 2 165

Adverbs

Types of Adverbs 167
Forms of Adverbs 169

Prepositions

Prepositional Phrases 171

Interjections

Interjections 173

Conjunctions

Coordinating Conjunctions 175
Subordinating Conjunctions 177
Conjunctions Review 179

Parts of Speech

Parts of Speech Review 1, 2, and 3 180

Proofreading Activities

The activities in this section include sentences that need to be checked for punctuation, mechanics, spelling, or correct word choices. Most of the activities also include helpful *Write Source* references. In addition, the **Next Step** activities encourage follow-up practice of certain skills.

Marking Punctuation 3

Editing for Mechanics 41

Improving Spelling 51

Using the Right Word 53

End Punctuation 1

Periods, exclamation points, and question marks are used at the ends of sentences. Usually, these marks will mean that you have come to the end of a complete thought—either a statement or a question. (See 579.1, 580.1, and 580.4 in *Write Source* for more information.)

Examples

People must sleep to stay healthy.
(A period marks the end of a complete thought.)

How many hours of sleep do we need each day?
(A question mark indicates a question.)

My older brother once slept for 12 straight hours!
(An exclamation point expresses strong feelings or emphasis.)

Directions **Put periods, question marks, and exclamation points where they are needed in the following paragraphs. Also supply the needed capital letters at the beginnings of sentences. The first one has been done for you.**

You know, of course, that people need to sleep have you ever heard that if you work hard during the day, you'll sleep well during the night

Actually, there is another reason for sleep scientists now feel that the need for sleep goes beyond your physical state your brain needs sleep, too, and it will not function normally for long without sleep it is now known that people need to dream in order to maintain healthy brains

Scientists have found that everyone dreams if people do not dream, their brains will stop working normally if you go without dreaming, you will become upset very easily after a while, you may even suffer memory loss the effects of dreamlessness may last for weeks or months just think about that

Why is dreaming so necessary scientists are not sure of the answer during sleep, the brain really doesn't rest it is very active all night long the brain needs the special kind of activity it gets while you sleep

You need to help your brain function properly don't stay up late to watch TV or do homework do some good dreaming instead

Next Step Write a paragraph about a time when you were really tired, but you had to stay awake. Use all three kinds of end punctuation in your paragraph—periods, question marks, and exclamation points.

End Punctuation 2

Periods, question marks, and exclamation points are used to mark the ends of sentences; but periods have other uses also. (See page 579 and 600.1 in *Write Source* for all the rules covering periods.)

Directions **Place periods, question marks, and exclamation points where they belong in the following narrative. Add capital letters to the beginnings of sentences. The first sentence has been done for you.**

did you know that the world's largest animal lives in the water it's the blue whale this type of whale generally weighs 110 to 150 tons that's heavier than the biggest dinosaur that ever lived Peter J Fromm tells some amazing stories about this gentle giant in his book *Whale Tales: Human Interaction with Whales*

The blue whale can survive for six months without eating a thing how does it do that it lives off its own blubber wouldn't you think that this huge creature would go after a shark or an octopus when it is hungry no, the blue whale exists almost completely on a diet of shrimp-like animals called krill

Endangered whales include blue whales, humpback whales, fin whales, and sperm whales in the 1970s an organization called Greenpeace drew attention to the plight of whales everywhere this organization tried to get whaling stopped how did they do this

Greenpeace created media stunts they placed a small inflatable lifeboat between a large whaling vessel and the whale it was hunting this made great pictures for television and newspapers and got many people on the whales' side

"Save the whales" became a common battle cry people who hadn't thought much about whales before joined the crusade bumper stickers carried the message across the country

All of this publicity led to a ban on commercial whaling for five years not every country agreed to the ban, but whaling was dramatically decreased the gigantic blue whale now has a chance to be around for many centuries hurrah for the whales

Next Step Whales, elephants, and cattle have the same names for the male, female, and young of their species. Without researching the topic, write a paragraph that explains why *you* think these three species share names.

Commas Between Items in a Series

Commas are used to separate a series of three or more words, phrases, or clauses. They are also used in big numbers. (See 582.1 and 582.2 in *Write Source* for more information and examples.)

Examples

Sand is made up of tiny pieces of rocks, shells, and lava.
(Commas are used to separate words in a series.)

Strong winds, pounding waves, and changing temperatures gradually turn rocks into sand.
(Commas are used to separate phrases in a series.)

Waves pound against the coastline, water freezes in the cracks of the rocks, and the rocks split apart.
(Commas are used to separate clauses in a series.)

Collecting 1,000,000 sand dollars won't make you rich.
(Commas are used to keep big numbers clear.)

Directions **Use commas correctly in the sentences below. The first sentence has been done for you.**

1. The five largest deserts in the world are the Sahara, the Australian, the Arabian, the Gobi, and the Kalahari.
2. These deserts are found in Africa, Australia, Southwest Asia, and Central Asia.
3. The Sahara Desert covers 9,065,000 square kilometers, the Gobi Desert covers 1,295,000 square kilometers, and Death Valley in the United States covers only 13,500 square kilometers.
4. Deserts are made up of rocks, gravel, or sand.

5. Death Valley is the driest, hottest, and lowest place in North America.

6. Over the course of time, the Sahara has been covered by ice, seawater, forests, and grass.

7. Sandstorms have been known to whip up the sand as high as 1 0,0 0 0 feet with the power to sandblast the paint off a car, a truck, or an airplane.

8. The Gobi Desert is located on the border between China and Mongolia and lies on a plateau that is between 2,9 5 0 and 4,9 2 0 feet high.

9. Fossilized eggs, bones, and the skeleton of a giant tyrannosaur have been found in the Gobi Desert.

10. The world's deserts are growing because of improper farming, mining, and the destruction of trees.

Next Step What are the hottest places that you have ever lived in or visited? Write a sentence that includes a list of these places (punctuated with commas, of course). Then write a paragraph that describes one of these places using lists of words, phrases, and clauses.

Commas to Set Off Nonrestrictive Phrases and Clauses

A phrase or clause that is not needed to complete the meaning of a sentence is called a **nonrestrictive phrase** or **clause**. A nonrestrictive phrase or clause adds "extra" information and is set off with commas. A phrase or clause that is needed to complete the meaning of a sentence is called a **restrictive phrase** or **clause.** A restrictive phrase or clause is not set off with commas. (See 584.1 in *Write Source*.)

Examples

Nonrestrictive Phrase:

Many things, <u>from leaves to dinosaurs</u>, can become fossils.

(The underlined phrase is "nonrestrictive" because the meaning of the sentence is complete without it.)

Restrictive Clause:

Anything <u>that can be preserved for a long time</u> can become a fossil.

(The underlined clause is "restrictive" because the meaning of the sentence is not complete without it.)

This activity gives you practice identifying nonrestrictive and restrictive phrases and clauses. On the line before each sentence below, write whether the underlined phrase or clause is "nonrestrictive" or "restrictive." The first sentence has been done for you.

nonrestrictive **1.** Sharks, <u>which do not have bones</u>, rarely leave fossils.

restrictive **2.** The soft cartilage <u>that makes up sharks' skeletons</u> dissolves over time.

restrictive **3.** The only part of a shark <u>that lasts for millions of years</u> is its teeth!

nonrestrictive **4.** Recently scientists found the first fossils of Gigantosaurus, which means "monstrous lizard."

nonrestrictive **5.** Gigantosaurus, which lived in South America, was even bigger than Tyrannosaurus rex.

restrictive **6.** Rancho La Brea Tar Pit and Dinosaur National Monument are two places that have a lot of dinosaur fossils.

restrictive **7.** Many insects become fossilized when they get stuck in amber.

nonrestrictive **8.** David Shiffler, who was born in 1992, is already a famous fossil finder.

restrictive **9.** On a camping trip when he was three, David found something that he thought was a dinosaur egg.

nonrestrictive **10.** David's father didn't believe him, but David was right, according to a fossil expert.

restrictive **11.** Emily Bray, a fossil expert, said the egg that David found was 150 million years old.

Next Step Each sentence below has one nonrestrictive phrase or clause and one restrictive phrase or clause. Write "N" above each nonrestrictive phrase or clause and "R" above each restrictive phrase or clause.

1. Petoskey stones, (N) which are found in Petoskey, Michigan, have fossils (R) that can only be seen when the stones are wet.

2. Explorers Lewis and Clark, (N) when they were in Montana, found dinosaur bones (R) that they thought were the bones of huge elephants.

Commas to Set Off Explanatory Phrases

Commas are used to set off phrases that rename or explain nouns. (See 586.1 and 588.4 in *Write Source* for more information.)

Examples

The rattlesnake, a poisonous snake common in the United States, rattles its tail when a person or an animal gets too close.
(Commas separate an appositive from the rest of the sentence. An appositive renames the noun it follows.)

Snakes, legless reptiles located on most continents, are affected by the temperature of the air and the ground.
(Commas are used to separate an explanatory phrase from the rest of the sentence.)

Directions Add commas to the sentences below. If a sentence is already correct, write "correct" on the line. The first sentence has been done for you.

1. ________ There are two types of snakes poisonous and nonpoisonous.
2. ________ The water moccasin a poisonous snake found in southern swamps is known for its dark body and white mouth.
3. ________ Although many people are afraid of snakes, these animals which are actually very timid help control pest populations.
4. ________ Certain snakes use poison to kill rats and mice their main food source.
5. ________ All snakes poisonous and nonpoisonous have scales on their bodies.
6. ________ Wider scales which are found on the belly of a snake are used to move it forward.

7. ________ The scales must push against the ground so that a snake can move, so a snake is helpless on glass a very smooth material.

8. ________ In northern states, the garter snake a harmless yellow-and-black-striped reptile is often found in backyards.

9. correct Never pick up poisonous snakes, which have heads shaped like arrowheads.

10. ________ In the Southwest, the sidewinder a snake that lives in the desert moves sideways by touching only two points of its body to the ground to avoid being burned by hot sand.

11. ________ Although the blue racer a snake of meadows and forests sounds like a fast-moving snake, it can only go four miles an hour.

12. ________ The royal python which has bright colors and is very popular with pet owners will often curl itself into a ball when it is frightened.

13. ________ The left lung very small in some snakes is actually missing in many others.

14. correct There are no snakes in Ireland, an island near the western coast of Europe.

Next Step Write five sentences that contain appositives. Write about animals and facts you know about them. For example, *A dog, my favorite pet, is very loyal to its owner.* (Don't forget to use commas correctly.)

Commas to Separate Long Introductory Phrases and Clauses

Commas are used to separate long phrases and clauses from the rest of a sentence. Commas are also used to separate two or more adjectives that equally modify the same noun. (See 586.2 and 590.1 in *Write Source* for more information.)

Examples

After a long period of time, the origin of a piece of music is often forgotten.
(A comma is placed after a long introductory phrase.)

When people write classical music, they are called composers.
(A comma is placed after an introductory clause.)

Not all composers are trained, professional musicians.
(Place commas between two or more adjectives that equally describe the same noun.)

Add commas to the following sentences. If the sentence is already correct, write "correct" on the line. The first sentence has been done for you.

1. ________ Although you may find it hard to believe, "Chopsticks" was actually composed by someone.
2. ________ Loud, pounding versions of "Chopsticks" have been played by many beginning pianists.
3. ________ The person who created "Chopsticks" was a talented, high-strung teenager from Great Britain named Euphemia Allen.
4. ________ When the tune first appeared in 1877, it was called "The Celebrated Chopsticks Waltz, Arranged as a Duet and Solo for the Pianoforte."

5. _________ Then the long,complicated name of the piece was shortened to simply "Chopsticks."

6. correct The term "pianoforte" is just a fancy name for "piano."

7. _________ You might think that "Chopsticks" was named after the long,thin eating utensils used by the Chinese.

8. _________ As a matter of fact,the name "Chopsticks" comes from the chopping motion the fingers make while playing this music.

9. _________ At the time that Euphemia wrote her "masterpiece," one-finger piano pieces were popular with children.

10. _________ Little did she know that she was composing such a timeless,universal piece of music.

Next Step Write a paragraph that explains how to play a musical instrument, a sport, or a game. Use at least two long introductory phrases or clauses ("Before you pick up the bat, . . . " or "After placing both hands on the keyboard, . . . ") in your paragraph.

Commas in Compound Sentences

A comma is used between two independent clauses that are joined by a coordinating conjunction. (See 590.2 in *Write Source* for more information.)

Example

People have always dreamed of flying, but the earliest recorded flight took place in 1793.
(A comma is used between two independent clauses joined by the coordinating conjunction "but.")

Add commas to the sentences below. The first sentence has been done for you.

1. The Montgolfier brothers were the first to fly in a hot-air balloon, and people were astonished.
2. No one thought the Wright brothers' flying machine would work, but that didn't stop the brothers from trying.
3. Their airplane was called *Flyer I*, and it flew for a full 12 seconds.
4. *Flyer I* flew less than 100 feet, yet it put the Wright brothers in the history books.
5. At one time, the Concorde aircraft flew at twice the speed of sound, and it crossed the Atlantic in less than three hours.
6. Each year, nearly a billion people fly on airplanes, and that's just on commercial flights.
7. Now it's possible to "fly" anywhere in the world, and you do it on the Internet.

Directions Complete the following sentences with a comma, a conjunction, and a second independent clause. The first one has been done for you.

(Answers will vary.)

1. Neither the Montgolfier brothers nor the Wright brothers would believe it,

   but air travel is now a normal part of everyday life.

2. My brother has flown three times,

   and I hope to take my third flight this summer.

3. Flying is a very safe form of transportation,

   yet there can still be accidents.

4. Most passenger planes do not fly faster than the speed of sound,

   but someday that may change.

5. Some big planes hold more than 350 people,

   but I have flown only in small planes.

6. Stunt flying seems very scary,

   yet some people make a living that way.

Next Step Write a paragraph about some other form of transportation. Use at least three compound sentences (independent clauses joined by commas and coordinating conjunctions).

Comma Practice 1

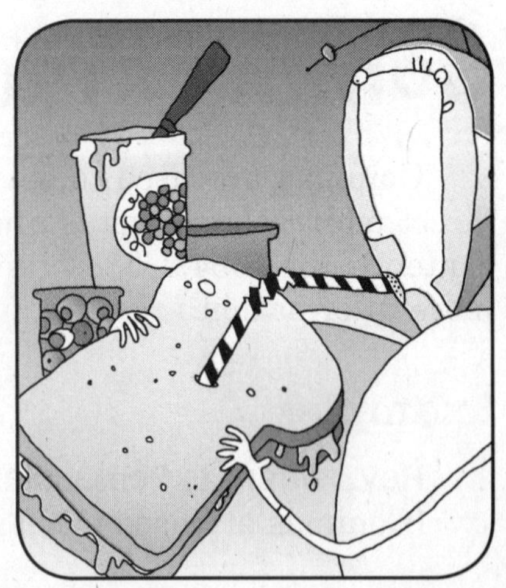

Commas are used to separate words, phrases, or clauses in sentences. Commas make writing easier to read. (See pages 582–590 in *Write Source*.)

Examples

After I drank the entire quart of orange juice, my stomach felt kind of queasy.
(The comma after "juice" separates an adverb clause from the main sentence, or independent clause, that follows it.)

I like grape jam, cream cheese, and green olives on a sandwich.
(The commas separate a series of words.)

My brother likes peanut-butter sandwiches, but I think they're boring.
(The comma separates two independent clauses.)

Read the paragraph that follows and add commas where you think they are needed. Use the examples above as your guide.

I use a computer for producing final drafts, but I can't actually write on it. I turn it on, listen to it boot up, put my fingers on the keyboard, and then . . . nothing. On the other hand, writing on paper makes me feel as if I can conquer the whole world. When I see the ink on the page, I know I'm making my mark. The words are like clay in my hands, and I can rework them until they're right. I may change words two, three, or four times before I am satisfied. On the computer screen, words seem to be written in stone. They stare out at me, and I find it difficult to work with them.

Next Step Exchange your work with a classmate and check each other's work. If you have questions, refer to *Write Source*.

Comma Practice 2

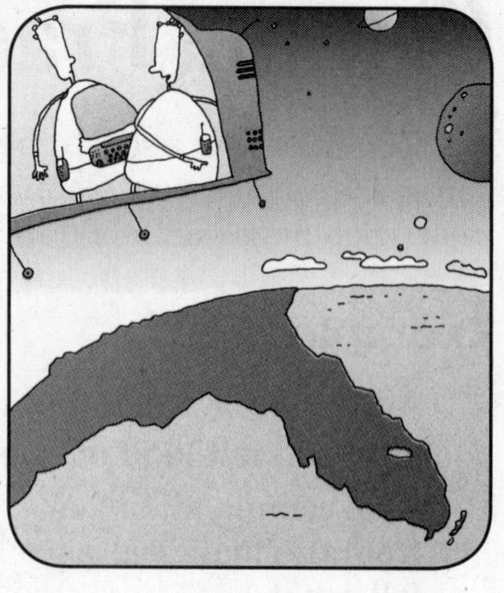

Commas are used to set off interjections, nouns of direct address, and words and phrases that interrupt a sentence. (See 584.3, 588.2, and 588.3 in *Write Source* for more information.)

Examples

Hey, where is Pensacola?
(Commas are used to set off interjections.)

Jim, Pensacola is in Florida.
(Commas are used to set off nouns of direct address.)

More specifically, Pensacola is in the Florida panhandle.
(Commas are used to set off a word, phrase, or clause that introduces a sentence.)

Add commas to the sentences below. The first sentence has been done for you.

"Jim, have you ever heard of a city named Peculiar in Missouri?"

"No, I've heard of Normal, Illinois, but not Peculiar, Missouri."

"As a matter of fact, Jim, lots of U.S. towns have unusual names."

"Yes, I know. For example, there's a town called Why in Arizona."

"Hmm, that's pretty close to Whynot, Mississippi."

"Right, Joe. Do you think it's safe to live in Accident, Maryland?"

"Hey, I wouldn't risk it. By the way, I wonder if all the folks in Library, Pennsylvania, and in Magazine, Arkansas, are good readers."

Next Step Continue this conversation between Joe and Jim. Add two more sentences with funny or interesting place names. Use direct address *(Joe, Jim),* interrupters *(for example),* and interjections *(hey, no kidding).*

Comma Practice 3

Here's a chance for you to practice four important uses of commas. Review the examples below before you begin your work. (Also see 582.1, 584.3, and 590.1–590.2 in *Write Source* for more examples.)

Examples

(A) A comma is used between two independent clauses connected with a coordinating conjunction (a compound sentence):
I work very hard from Monday through Friday, but I enjoy myself on weekends.

(B) Commas separate items in a series:
Attending school, going to soccer practice, and completing homework take up all of my time during the week.

(C) A comma separates a long introductory phrase or clause from the rest of the sentence:
When Friday night arrives, I'm totally exhausted.

(D) Commas set off phrases that interrupt the main thought:
I'm so tired, in fact, that I usually fall asleep really early.

Directions **Find the rule ("A," "B," "C," or "D") that applies to the commas used in the first six sentences below. Then write the correct letter on each line. For the last five sentences, you must supply both the commas and the letters. The first sentence has been done for you.**

1. B I like shopping, reading, and playing badminton on weekends.

2. D My mother, on the other hand, loves to take piles of work home with her.

3. A I would love to go to the movies, but I have my final soccer match.

4. C When I wake up on Saturday morning, I head straight for the sweet rolls in the kitchen.

5. B I have to pick up my room, clear the kitchen table, and walk the dog before I can go out.

6. C Although Josie is my best friend at school, I do more things with Anna on weekends.

7. C When I see blue sky through my window, I always feel like smiling.

8. B Lawrence could finally catch his breath after taking a shower, rushing through breakfast, and running to his game.

9. D Jackie watched three movies, believe it or not, before she developed a major headache.

10. A My mother often tells me I'm pretty, yet I try to hide behind my hair.

11. C In the last part of fall, I like to rake up huge piles of leaves and jump in them.

Directions Write original sentences according to the directions provided below. (Make sure to use commas correctly in your sentences.)

(Answers will vary.)

1. Write a compound sentence using the connecting word *but.*

   I'm not really hungry, but I can't stop eating these crackers.

2. Write a sentence that includes a series of words or phrases.

   I have to go to the doctor, change my clothes, and dash off to the party.

3. Write a sentence that includes a long introductory phrase or clause.

   Once I eat one Bing cherry, I can't stop eating a whole bunch more.

4. Write a sentence that includes a phrase that interrupts the sentence's main thought.

   Liver and onions, on the other hand, aren't nearly as tempting.

Semicolons and Colons

Both semicolons and colons have several uses, including the ones shown in the examples below. Study these examples and the ones in *Write Source* (pages 594 and 596) before you start your work.

Examples

Quartz is the most common mineral found in the world; ordinary sand is made up mostly of quartz.
(A semicolon can be used to join two independent clauses that are not connected with a coordinating conjunction—"and," "or," "but.")

There are many varieties of quartz: agate, amethyst, flint, jasper, onyx.
(A colon can be used to introduce a list.)

Quartz is a very hard mineral; however, it is not as hard as diamond.
(A semicolon is used to join two independent clauses when the clauses are connected by a conjunctive adverb—"however," "therefore," "as a result," "for example," and so on.)

A geologist named David Vister stated this fact: "Erosion does not wear away quartz as rapidly as most other rock materials."
(A colon may be used to formally introduce a quotation.)

Add semicolons and colons to the sentences below. The first sentence has been done for you.

1. The earth contains many kinds of minerals; moreover, some of the same minerals have been found on the moon, on other planets, and in meteorites.
2. Quartz is used in making the following items: watches and clocks, heat-resistant glass, microscope lenses, and sandpaper.
3. Minerals are solid, nonliving materials in the soil; rocks are combinations of minerals.

4. There are three kinds of rocks: igneous, sedimentary, and metamorphic.

5. Granite, marble, and quartzite are considered hard rocks; limestone, sand, and shale are considered soft rocks.

6. Geologists study rocks by drilling deep into the crust of the earth; they also use aerial photography and satellites to get information about the earth's surface.

7. Not every precious gem comes from minerals; for example, pearls come from oysters, which are living things.

8. The most precious stones are the following: emeralds, rubies, sapphires, and diamonds.

9. Both diamonds and graphite pencils are made of carbon; however, diamonds are certainly much more valuable.

10. Mrs. MacIntosh made this claim: "I love carbon. I never go anywhere without my diamond ring or my pencil."

Next Step Have you ever noticed how many things are made of cement—pulverized minerals mixed with sand? Write a paragraph in which you imagine a world without cement. What would be missing? How would your life be different? Use at least one colon to introduce a list, and a semicolon to join two independent clauses.

Punctuating Dialogue 1

A conversation in writing is called *dialogue*. There are special rules for using quotation marks, commas, and end punctuation marks when you are punctuating dialogue. (See 598.1 and 600.1 in *Write Source* for more information.)

Examples

"I'm bored," said Clara. "Let's go shopping."
(A period comes after "Clara" because that's the end of a complete sentence.)

"Oh yeah," replied Sue, "there's a great sale at the mall."
(A comma comes after "Sue" because what follows completes the sentence.)

"Let's go now, Sue!" Clara yelled.
(The exclamation point is inside the quotation marks because the quotation is an exclamation.)

Directions

Punctuate the following examples of dialogue with quotation marks, commas, and end marks. The first sentence has been done for you.

Hey, Joe, there's a bee on your back yelled Carlyle Hold still while I swish it away

Everyone be quiet and take your seats said Mr. Beech

But what about the bee said Joe I could be stung

Just sit still. It won't sting you if you stop jumping around advised Mr. Beech

It's a known fact added Carlyle that bees only sting if you scare them

Real funny, Carlyle. Now just get it off me pleaded Joe.

Punctuating Dialogue 2

When you are writing dialogue, you have to start a new paragraph each time the speaker in a conversation changes. (See 598.1, 598.2, and 600.1 in *Write Source* for more information.)

Directions **Add quotation marks, commas, and end punctuation as needed. The first sentence has been done for you.**

What's there to do around here José asked.

Why don't you do something to improve your mind suggested his father. Here's an article about native wildflowers that you could read

Uh, thanks, Dad José said That sounds fascinating

What about reading short stories such as A Start in Life from your literature text asked his mom. I'm sure you won't read them all in class

I've been dying to do that José said but I'm already trying to finish three chapters in my social studies book

You could attend a lecture at the community center his older brother volunteered. I heard that the basket weaving session is awesome.

You guys are really helpful said José but I have to go. I just remembered I have to watch a video I rented. See you later.

Next Step Re-create a conversation you recently had with someone. Make sure to punctuate the conversation correctly.

Quotation Marks and Italics

The titles of shorter pieces of writing (short stories, articles, songs, and so on) are placed in quotation marks, while the titles of longer pieces (books, magazines, CD's, and so on) are italicized. (See 600.3 and 602.3 in *Write Source* to review the rules about punctuating titles.)

Examples

"Another Time" received two Grammy awards.
(The song title is placed in quotation marks.)

Galactic Soup is my favorite book on the universe.
(The book title is underlined to show italics.)

In this exercise, add underlining (to show italics) and quotation marks. The first sentence has been done for you.

1. What were you doing on June 10, 2003, when the Mars rover Spirit was launched?
2. Opportunity, which was launched a couple weeks later, joined Spirit to look for signs of life.
3. I read an article in the Chicago Tribune entitled "NASA's Rover Touches Down Safely on Mars" that told how the rover landed on the surface of Mars.
4. A Canadian magazine, the Globe and Mail, reported Spirit landed after traveling 303 million miles over seven months.
5. An old Time for Kids magazine article, "A Mars Mission Ends," tells about the end of the Pathfinder mission.

6. My uncle told me about a novel called Red Mars that tells a story about colonizing Mars.

7. Our teacher read part of a chapter in Hunt for Life on Mars called "Origin of Life."

8. Discovery magazine published an article about the Martian canals entitled "Ole Mars River."

9. Popular movies like The Red Planet show that people still enjoy science fiction.

10. The 1960s TV series Twilight Zone featured many stories about life in outer space, including "People Are Alike All Over," which tells about a trip to Mars.

11. Maybe someday I will pick up a National Geographic magazine to read an article entitled "How Settlers Are Living on Mars."

Next Step What good-news headlines would you like to see in the newspaper? Think about it and then write a sentence containing three headlines that would make your day. Use quotation marks correctly.

Apostrophes 1

Apostrophes are used to form contractions, to show ownership or possession, and for other special uses. (See pages 604 and 606 in *Write Source* for more examples and explanations.)

Examples

To Form Contractions:
isn't (is + not) **we're (we + are)**

To Form Singular Possessives:
Carey's shoes **my aunt's sunflower book**

To Form Plural Possessives:
the teachers' meeting **the women's department**

To Show Shared Possession:
Tim and Janna's cat **the girls' volleyball**

Directions **Add apostrophes as needed in the following sentences. The first sentence has been done for you.**

1. Tamaras brother Theo rode her bike and didnt put it away.
2. Katy and Matties mural shows our towns most well-known sights.
3. Ben has three beagles, and you should see those dogs ears when a siren sounds.
4. Tony said he would take everybodys books back to the library, but he couldnt do it until Friday.
5. We have to learn all the planets names and their distances from the sun.
6. Jill cant go to the movies because today is her parents anniversary.
7. Our teachers favorite book is *Old Possums Book of Practical Cats.*
8. I promised to take care of Lee McLeans cats while shes on vacation.

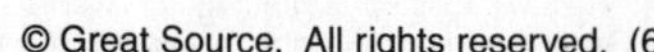

Directions **In the story below, put a line through each underlined word that has an apostrophe error. Then correct the error. The first underlined word has been checked and corrected for you. *Hint:* An additional five underlined words contain apostrophe errors.**

William Tell was a hero who lived in Switzerland ~~hundred's~~ hundreds of years ago. William's courage and his ability as an archer were widely known. He often spoke out against the cruel emperor and ignored the man's orders. One day, the ~~emperors'~~ emperor's patience ran out, and he had William jailed.

"Since ~~youre~~ you're such a brave man and a great marksman," the emperor said, "I'll give you a chance to win your freedom. If you can shoot an apple off your young ~~sons~~ son's head, you'll be free."

Of course, William refused. But the emperor said that if William wouldn't take the challenge, both he and his son would be killed.

The whole town held its breath as ~~Williams~~ William's son stood against a tree and William took aim at the apple. When the arrow pinned the apple to the tree, the people's cheers could be heard for miles. The emperor asked William why he had arrived with two ~~arrows'~~ arrows in his belt, one of which remained there.

"If the first arrow had touched my son's head," said William Tell, "the second would have pierced your heart."

Apostrophes 2

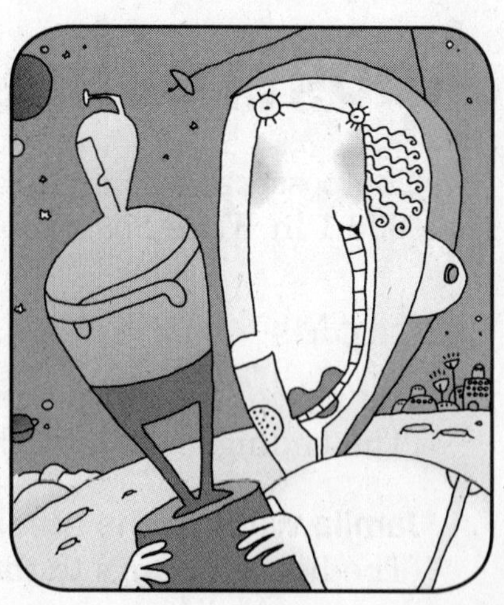

The possessive of most singular nouns is formed by adding an apostrophe and *s.* (See 604.4 in *Write Source* for more information.)

Examples

Susan's trophy is at my house.
(The trophy belongs to Susan.)

I changed the story's ending.
(The ending belongs to the story.)

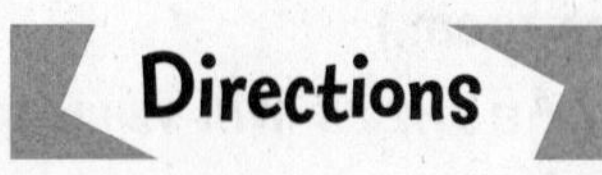

Use the singular possessive form of each of the following words in a sentence. (Use your own paper if you need more room.)

(Answers will vary.)

1. clock ______________________________

____

2. friend ______________________________

____

3. monkey ______________________________

____

4. ______________ (name of a favorite character in a book or story)

____

____

5. ______________ (name of a favorite movie or sports star) ______________

____

____

Apostrophes 3

The possessive of a plural noun that ends in *s* is formed by adding an apostrophe. (See 606.1 in *Write Source* for more information.)

Examples

The stories' endings were exactly the same.
(The endings belong to the stories.)

Jamila went to the Greens' house.
(The house belongs to the Greens.)

Use the plural possessive form of each of the following words in a sentence. (Use your own paper if you need more room.)

(Answers will vary.)

1. trees ______________________________

2. Smiths ______________________________

3. bugs ______________________________

4. ______________ (name of a favorite sports team) ______________

5. ______________ (name of a family you know) ______________

Hyphens and Dashes

Hyphens are used to divide a word between its syllables and to join words for different reasons. **Dashes** are used to show a sudden break or interruption in a sentence and to emphasize a word, a phrase, or a clause. Study the examples below plus the ones at 608.1–610.3, and 612.1–612.3 in *Write Source* before you work on this activity.

Examples

My all-time record for a grocery purchase was three and one-half seconds.
(Hyphens are used to join two or more words used as a single adjective. They are also used in spelled-out fractions.)

I bought a pack of gum—I think it was gum—at the store.
(Dashes are used to show an interruption in a sentence.)

My pet peeve is waiting—waiting for supper, waiting for tickets, waiting at checkout counters.
(A dash can be used to emphasize the words that follow.)

Add hyphens and dashes to the paragraphs that follow. The first sentence has been done for you.

Now, I'm not one to complain about high tech gadgets. I'm a red blooded, all American girl. I love computers and anything that will save me three fourths of a second. While my mother bless her heart stands in an actual line to check out books at the library, I zip my library card through the self scanner. She says she doesn't trust the scanner, but I think she's just old fashioned and worried that she won't do it right.

Now, self scanning devices, which were introduced in 1998, are in almost every store. Storekeepers say that scanning provides hassle-free shopping.

When customers finally make their decisions, they don't want to wait in mile-long lines just to pay for their purchases. You scan your own purchases, drop them into a bag, get a receipt, and then get in line to pay a cashier. (This line—thankfully, a very short one—moves quickly.)

The scanner even prevents not-so-honest customers from dropping little "extras" into their bags. It checks to see that everything you drop into your store-provided bag matches the weight—down to the last milligram—of the item you just scanned. Satisfied customers—and that's what we all want to be—say scanning offers the quickest shopping experience ever. There is just one thing that I wonder about. What will we do with all the minutes—maybe even hours—that we save?

Next Step Write a paragraph about a recent shopping experience. Use at least one set of dashes and one hyphen in your work. Afterward, share your writing with a classmate. Check each other's use of these two marks of punctuation.

Punctuation Review 1

Directions **Add missing commas and end punctuation to the following passage. Also add capital letters as necessary. The first sentence has been corrected for you. (See pages 579–612 in *Write Source*.)**

Did you know that Ellis Island was the chief immigration station for the United States between 1892 and 1954 in fact nearly 15000000 people entered the United States through Ellis Island, in the early years the majority of the immigrants came from European countries, such as Great Britain, Ireland Italy Russia and Germany.

Ellis Island nicknamed "Heartbreak Island" stood between the immigrants and the new country in a huge inspection room with iron dividers the newcomers were examined by two doctors if the first doctor spotted an obvious physical mental or social problem he put a chalk mark on the person's right shoulder the second doctor looked for diseases and infections have you ever heard of trachoma it is a serious eye disease the second doctor would look for

Each immigrant was then questioned every family worried that a family member would be rejected and he or she would have to return home what a horrible thing to have happen most immigrants passed through Ellis Island in about a day but some people had to wait as long as three days

California has the most new immigrants with New York, Florida, Texas, New Jersey and Illinois following behind Europe is no longer the largest source of immigrants the top six countries for U.S. immigrants in 2003 were Mexico the Philippines India Vietnam China and the Dominican Republic they represented well over a third (40.4 percent) of the total immigrants in that year

Next Step Some people know a little about their family history, and some people know a lot—but everyone knows something. Write a paragraph that tells something interesting about your family history.

Punctuation Review 2

There are times when writers need more than commas and end marks to keep their writing clear. In such cases, they use semicolons, colons, dashes, or hyphens.

To complete the activity below, remember that . . .

> **semicolons** are used before conjunctive adverbs such as "however," and to join two independent clauses.
>
> **colons** are used to introduce a list or to introduce a formal quotation.
>
> **dashes** are used to show a sudden break in a sentence.
>
> **hyphens** are used to join two words.

Punctuate the following sentences correctly. The first sentence has been done for you. (See pages 579–612 in *Write Source*.)

1. There are four foods I don't like oysters, liver, fish, and peas.
2. I'm in the mood for a large six topping pizza.
3. My dog is the cutest pet in the world she is all fluffy and white with a black patch around one eye.
4. I wanted to name my dog Scooter however, I was overruled by my mother, who named her Helga.
5. Someone should invent self polishing shoes.
6. The teacher gave us another five paragraph assignment.
7. I know what I want for a present a new jacket.
8. When I asked my dad if I could go to a movie, I got the usual response "Not on a school night."
9. I pleaded with my dad actually I begged but he wouldn't change his mind.

Directions **Carefully read the paragraph below, paying special attention to the underlined words. Put a line through any word that contains an apostrophe error and write the correct form above it. The first two underlined words have been checked for you.**
***Hint:* Five of the underlined words (including the one corrected for you) contain apostrophe errors.**

When I was little, I used to bake cookies at my grandmother's house all the time. My favorite kind was chocolate chip, but we also baked a lot of peanut-butter cookies. They were my ~~grandpas'~~ grandpa's favorite. Whenever it rained, my grandmother would call over to my house and say, "Looks like it's a good day for baking." I'd put on my raincoat, borrow my ~~brothers'~~ brother's bike, and ride over to my grandparents' house. (My ~~bikes'~~ bike's tires always seemed to be flat.) Once there, I'd immediately turn on the oven and keep checking ~~it's~~ its temperature while Grandma cracked the eggs. ~~Grandpas'~~ Grandpa's eyes looked a little disappointed when he saw we were making chocolate-chip cookies. Maybe someday I'll bake all of my relatives' favorite cookies.

Next Step Write a paragraph about a pleasant memory of a grandparent or some other adult. (Use the paragraph above as a model.) Before you share your results with a classmate, check your writing for punctuation errors.

Punctuation Review 3

Directions **Proofread the paragraphs below. Delete any mark of punctuation or capital letter that is used incorrectly. Then add any punctuation or capital letters that are needed. The first two errors have been corrected for you. (See pages 579–612 in *Write Source*.)**

Imagine yourself sitting in your, living room watching TV. Before you can turn your head oil starts gushing through the windows. Pretty soon your whole house is covered with oil. In addition, black sticky oil is all over you. Its in your mouth in your ears, and in your hair. You can't breathe, without getting it in your nose, and theres no clean place in the house where you can go to get away from the stuff

This is just what happened in 1989 to the fish birds and other animals that call Alaska their home. An oil tanker called the Exxon Valdez hit a reef in Prince William Sound. The ships' side had a huge hole ripped in it and the oil inside began spilling out. By the time the spill was stopped; 10 million gallons of crude oil had escaped into the ocean.

The massive oil slick then headed for shore fish were poisoned, and seals were left with nothing to eat. Birds who tried to fish for food were covered with terrible black guck. They couldn't preen themselves clean and they couldn't fly to clean water. Even if the birds could have gotten to clean water it wouldn't have done them any good oil doesnt just rinse off. Scientists figured it would take a billion dollars to clean up the oil spill, but now some think the affected area will never return to normal. The cost's are so high that a portion of the mess will probably just be forgotten and left there.

Unfortunately it will be a long time before wildlife will be able to live along some of the affected shoreline

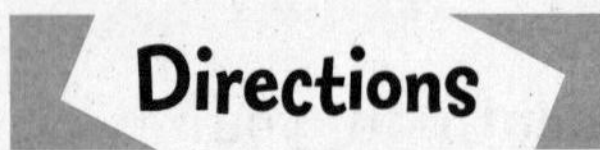

Work with a classmate, comparing your work before you turn it in. Discuss any differences, and look up your questions in the punctuation section of *Write Source*.

Next Step Write a descriptive paragraph about the oil spill from a seal's point of view. Here's a possible starting point:

I was basking on the beach when all of a sudden . . .

Mixed Review

Directions **The following paragraphs are missing many types of punctuation: periods, commas, a colon, hyphens, quotation marks, an apostrophe, and italics. Proofread the article carefully, adding the missing punctuation and any necessary capital letters. Double-check your work. *Note:* The actual name of the group in this activity—Boys Choir of Harlem—doesn't need an apostrophe. (See pages 579–612 in *Write Source*.)**

One of the most famous choirs in the United States is probably the Boys Choir of Harlem it was awarded the National Medal of the Arts by President Clinton in 1996 organized as a small boys' choir in the basement of a church the world famous Boys Choir of Harlem now gives 125 performances around the world each year.

The genius behind the choir is Dr Walter Turnbull a master teacher and mentor Turnbull has been the choir director for its entire lifetime and he has set high standards for each of the 40 boys in the choir. In the book Lift Every Voice that he co-authored with Howard Manly, he says set goals and complete them the combination of talent, discipline and hard work is unbeatable."

The choir sings a variety of music classical modern gospel and jazz more than 2000 boys audition for the choir each year forty boys are chosen from a 250 member concert choir to sing in the touring choir and another 100 are in training for a year and a half

The choir has recorded many CDs such as Boys Choir of Harlem Holiday Album. This CD includes the traditional favorites Silent Night and Little Drummer Boy these young men are multitalented they might begin the evening with Bach and end with a self styled rap people are surprised to learn that we do more than just gospel says Turnbull we do all kinds of music.

Next Step Write a paragraph in which you describe an experience you have had as a singer or performer—in school, at home, or on the playground. When you have finished, exchange papers with a classmate and proofread each other's papers for punctuation errors.

Capitalization 1

You already know that you must capitalize the first word in a sentence. You also know about capitalizing the specific names of people and places. But there are additional rules for capitalization that you should know. For example, you must capitalize names of languages, races, nationalities, and religions. You must also capitalize the names of historical events and organizations. (See pages 618–626 in *Write Source* for more information about capitalization.)

In the following sentences, find the words that should be capitalized. Cross out the lowercase letters and write capital letters above them where needed. The first sentence has been done for you.

1. Rock and roll music came on the scene in the mid to late 1950s in places like new york city; kingston, jamaica; and liverpool, england.

2. Early rock and roll musicians such as elvis presley and little richard became international stars.

3. They influenced the next generations of musicians—including bruce springsteen and the rolling stones—throughout the United States and across the atlantic.

4. On the shores of lake erie in downtown cleveland, ohio, at 1040 east ninth street, there's an interesting tourist attraction: the rock and roll hall of fame and museum.

5. It opened in september of 1995 and was designed by world-famous architect i. m. pei, who also redesigned the louvre museum in paris, france.

6. The ahmet m. ertegus exhibit hall, the museum's main hall, is named after the son of the turkish ambassador to the united states; ahmet was the cofounder of atlantic records in 1947.

7. The museum features such famous performers as the beatles, tina turner, and aerosmith.

8. A 25,000-song database jukebox plays everything from chuck berry's "maybellene" to led zeppelin's "stairway to heaven."

9. In 2003, an exhibit called "respect: the sound of soul" featured african american singers like aretha franklin.

10. In *billboard* magazine, there is a weekly column, "chart beat," that answers readers' questions and provides information about performers.

11. In *billboard* magazine, you can read about the latest singers as well as longtime performers such as bonjovi.

12. Wouldn't if be fun to take a museum course with a title like "the roots of rock and roll"?

Next Step Write a paragraph about your favorite musician (or musical group). Answer the following types of questions in your writing: Why do you like this musician? What are your favorite songs? Have you ever seen the person or group perform?

Capitalization 2

Directions **The following paragraphs have capital letters only at the beginnings of sentences. Supply all of the other capital letters that are needed. (See pages 618–626 in *Write Source* for help.) The first sentence has been done for you.**

In 1803, the u.s. senate approved an incredible deal. It approved a treaty that allowed the united states to buy the enormous louisiana territory for 15 million dollars from france. Only 22 years had passed since the revolutionary war. The u.s. constitution was only 16 years old. The country was young—and small—compared to today.

The louisiana purchase, as it was called, came as a surprise. All or parts of this territory had been traded among the french, spanish, and english for a hundred years. The territory had been home to countless native american people for thousands of years. Through his minister of foreign affairs, napoleon, the emperor of france, made a deal with the americans for this territory.

Take a look at what was included in the 15 million-dollar purchase price: the present-day states of missouri, arkansas, iowa, minnesota west of the mississippi river, north dakota, south dakota, nebraska, oklahoma, most of kansas, montana, wyoming, colorado east of the rocky mountains, and the part of louisiana that is west of the mississippi. The city of new orleans was also thrown in. For little more than 1 million dollars per state, the united states suddenly doubled in size!

President thomas jefferson planned an expedition into the territory after reading a book in 1802 called *voyages from montreal.* Americans knew little about the interior of north america. Jefferson hoped someone would discover the northwest passage—a chain of lakes and rivers that people thought must connect the atlantic ocean to the pacific ocean. Jefferson also wanted to find a route for the pioneers who would be moving to the west.

Captain meriweather lewis and lieutenant william clark led the expedition. With 48 men they left st. louis, moved up the missouri river to north dakota, and then headed west, down the columbia river to what is now astoria, oregon. During their second season, they had the help of a shoshone guide named sakajawea.

The lewis and clark expedition never found the northwest passage (there isn't one), and they did not travel the route that became the oregon trail. They did, however, learn a great deal about the geography and the plant and animal life of the american west and midwest. They established peaceful relations, for the most part, with the native americans they met. When they came back from their 8,000-mile, two-and-a-half-year journey, they were greeted as true american heroes.

Next Step Find a topic that you know about or can find in your social studies text. Write a paragraph that explains why this event was important enough to include in a time line.

Capitalization and Abbreviations

When a sculptor creates a face out of a lump of clay, close attention is paid to every detail. The shape of the face must be carefully molded, and each of the face's features must be sculpted in just the right way. Writers are a lot like sculptors since they also must pay close attention to every detail. This includes carefully looking over a final draft, making sure every capital letter is in its proper place and every abbreviation is correctly written. (See pages 618–626, 634, and 636 in *Write Source* for the rules about using capital letters and abbreviations.)

Directions

Carefully read each sentence below. Put a line through any word or letter that is or is not capitalized or abbreviated correctly. Make corrections above each mistake. The first sentence has been done for you.

Hint: **Go through the activity once and fix everything you're sure about. Then use *Write Source* to help you with the tougher spots.**

1. last week, our class went to ocean city aquarium.
2. Our teacher, mr. tamillo, told us we would be going to the Arctic ocean Exhibit.
3. Joleen said, " i want to study the Penguins."
4. mike, Janelle, and al said they wanted to see the penguins, too.
5. We were surprised to see how big the Ocean City aquarium is.
6. mS Johnson, the tour guide, showed the class the first exhibit.
7. She carefully explained that this represented a small piece of the canadian northwest territories.
8. We were told that Moose, Caribou, and polar bears live in this kind of habitat.
9. Mr. Tamillo asked the guide, "do many people still survive by hunting these animals?"

10. Ms. johnson said that there are a few Groups who depend on hunting.

11. we learned that the arctic is mostly ocean and ice, so much of what we saw included water.

12. In fact, there is no such thing as a Continent or an Island known as the arctic.

13. We got to see Cormorants, fur Seals, narwhal whales, and seagulls.

14. A couple of large Dolphins jumped high above their tanks.

15. Ms. Johnson told us that explorers like dr. Robert E. Peary have helped answer scientists' questions about this remote area of the World.

16. One exhibit said that Pack Ice seems to be breaking up because of Global Warming.

17. In one area of the aquarium, we saw a gigantic tank filled with arctic fish such as Cod, Flounder, and Char.

18. some of those Arctic Fish were huge.

19. After lunch, Joleen asked ms. Johnson, "Where are the Penguins? I really want to see Penguins!"

20. Our guide said she had to answer her pager, but she pointed to a sign near the start of the Arctic Exhibit.

21. It read, "Many people come to the Ocean City Arctic exhibit hoping to see Penguins. No Penguins are here because Penguins do not live in the Arctic."

Next Step On your own paper, continue the story of the visit to the aquarium. Then exchange papers with a classmate and check each other's use of capitalization and abbreviations.

Plurals

To form the plural of most nouns you add an *s* or an *es* to the singular. But there are a few exceptions that you need to know. For example, the plural of some compound nouns is formed by adding *s* or *es* to the main word in the compound—as in *brothers-in-law.* Review all of the rules for forming plurals before you begin the activity below. (See pages 630 and 632 in *Write Source* for the rules and more examples of plurals.)

Directions **Write the plural form for each of the following singular nouns. The first one has been done for you.**

1.	armful	armfuls	**14.**	rodeo	rodeos
2.	ratio	ratios	**15.**	half	halves
3.	potato	potatoes	**16.**	belief	beliefs
4.	lady	ladies	**17.**	secretary of state	secretaries of state
5.	leaf	leaves	**18.**	elf	elves
6.	shovelful	shovelfuls	**19.**	alto	altos
7.	hoof	hooves	**20.**	stepsister	stepsisters
8.	mouse	mice	**21.**	father-in-law	fathers-in-law
9.	CD	CD's	**22.**	*A*	*A*'s
10.	passerby	passersby	**23.**	woman	women
11.	laboratory	laboratories	**24.**	duty	duties
12.	chief	chiefs	**25.**	4	4's
13.	hobby	hobbies	**26.**	bus	buses

Directions Rewrite each sentence below, changing the underlined phrase from singular to plural. The first sentence has been done for you.

1. May I have a French fry?

   May I have some French fries?

2. Kelly lost the key.

   Kelly lost the keys.

3. My cousin has a live turkey.

   My cousin has (some) live turkeys.

4. A man came to our classroom.

   (Two) men came to our classroom.

5. Sandy bought a dress.

   Sandy bought (three) dresses.

6. Keir drank a glassful of milk.

   Keir drank (two) glassfuls of milk.

7. Dara put a knife on the table.

   Dara put (the) knives on the table.

8. A branch fell on our house.

   (Some) branches fell on our house.

9. The deer ate from my hand.

   The deer ate from my hand.

10. My name has one *r*.

    My name has (two) r's.

Numbers

Some numbers should be written as words, and some numbers should be written as numerals. (See "Numbers," pages 638 and 640, in *Write Source* for explanations and examples.)

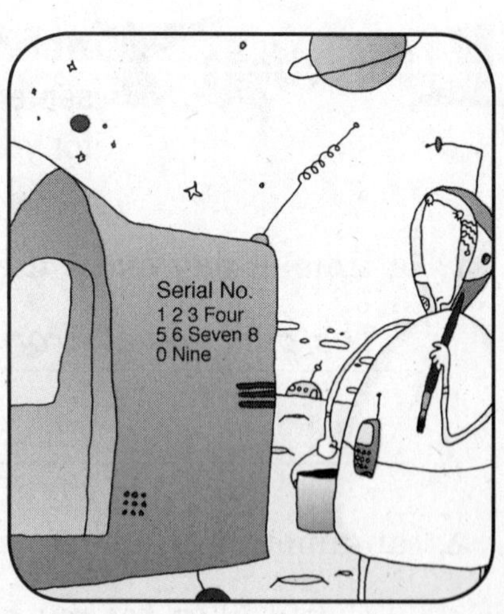

In the sentences below, all of the numbers are written as words. Find the number words that should be written as numerals and change them. The first sentence has been done for you.

1. Sally's brothers are ~~twelve~~ 12, ~~fourteen~~ 14, and ~~fifteen~~ 15.
2. We have to read chapters ~~one~~ 1 and ~~two~~ 2 by March ~~five~~ 5.
3. Chapter ~~two~~ 2 starts on page ~~thirty-two~~ 32.
4. Twenty-one students have spent a total of ~~two hundred and six~~ 206 hours doing volunteer work.
5. Jeremy has saved ~~42 dollars~~ $42 (or) forty-two dollars so far.
6. Jon got three books from the library that are due on July ~~sixteen~~ 16.
7. My sister has read eighteen ~~two hundred~~ 200-page books.
8. Mexico City has a population of nearly ~~twenty-five~~ 25 million.
9. I got this paperback on sale for ~~two dollars and fifty cents~~ $2.50.
10. The library opens at ~~eight-thirty~~ 8:30.
11. The players on his team range in age from nine to eleven. (or) 9 to 11

Write a sentence using each pair of numbers described below. Your sentences can be serious or silly. The first sentence has been done for you. *(Answers will vary.)*

1. a time of day and a day of the month

The party is at Tron's house at 12:00 p.m. on May 2.

2. an amount of money and a percentage

I paid $175 for my bike, which is about 50 percent of the regular price.

3. a street address and a highway number

Our school is located at 357 W. Oak Street, several blocks from Highway 88.

4. the number of students in your class and a percentage

Although there are 383 of us sixth graders, we make up only about 35 percent of the students in our school.

5. a date in history and a number in the millions

In 1950, the population of the United States numbered about 152 million.

Next Step Write two sentences that use numbers correctly. Each of your sentences should include at least one number written as a word and at least one number written as a numeral. (If you need ideas, look around at the people and things in your classroom.)

Spelling

You can avoid some spelling errors by learning a few basic spelling rules. (See page 642 and also review the plurals rules on pages 630 and 632 in *Write Source.*) As you will see, most of these rules deal with adding endings to words.

Read the sentences below and select the correctly spelled word to write in the blank. You will be able to make the correct choices by applying either the spelling rules or the plurals rules in *Write Source*. The first sentence has been done for you.

1. For my birthday, my mother made two huge (*loafs, loaves*) ___loaves___ of banana bread; each one (*wieghed, weighed*) ___weighed___ about two pounds.

2. As a gift I (*recieved, received*) ___received___ a beautiful book on (*ancient, anceint*) ___ancient___ Egypt.

3. I (*hurryed, hurried*) ___hurried___ through my (*nineth, ninth*) ___ninth___ piece of banana bread before I opened the book.

4. The (*beginning, begining*) ___beginning___ was about Egyptian writing, so I'll give you a little (*sumary, summary*) ___summary___ even if I can't (*truly, truely*) ___truly___ describe it all in so little space.

5. The Egyptians were a very religious people who had many (*preists, priests*) ___priests___, gods, and (*goddesses, godesses*) ___goddesses___ that they worshiped.

6. Specially trained people called scribes were the only ones who knew how to read and write the religious (*inscriptions, inscriptiones*) ___inscriptions___ .

7. The Egyptians' method of writing is known as (*heiroglyphics, hieroglyphics*) ___hieroglyphics___ .

8. The (*earlyest, earliest*) ___earliest___ writing was carved on stone, so I don't think they (*worryed, worried*) ___worried___ too much about typographical errors.

9. Hieroglyphics proved (*confuseing, confusing*) ___confusing___ to non-Egyptians because they didn't realize that the (*weird-looking, wierd-looking*) ___weird-looking___ marks could be read from left to right, right to left, or top to bottom.

10. In 1799, a (*soldeir, soldier*) ___soldier___ who was (*serving, serveing*) ___serving___ in Napoleon's army discovered the Rosetta stone, a stone tablet that had both Greek and hieroglyphic writing on it.

11. By (*refering, referring*) ___referring___ to the Greek script, which could be read, scientists finally broke the code and read hieroglyphics for the first time.

12. Although writing in hieroglyphics was (*neither, niether*) ___neither___ quick nor easy, it was used for more than 3,000 years on public monuments because it was (*decorateive, decorative*) ___decorative___ .

Next Step Ideograms are a form of hieroglyphics using pictures to send messages. (The following is a simple ideogram: 👁♡⚾.) Make up your own ideograms. Exchange some of your best ones with a classmate and see if you can figure out each other's messages.

Using the Right Word 1

Many writing errors are commonly made when one word is confused with another. Whenever you review your writing, pay close attention to the pairs or sets of words that often confuse you. Make sure to refer to "Using the Right Word" in the "Proofreader's Guide" whenever you have a usage question. (See pages 652–658 in *Write Source* for information on words in this exercise.)

Examples

I will accept your apology.
Everyone except Todd is tired.

I sat between Regie and Al.
We sat among many others.

A number of us had pancakes.
What amount of syrup did we use?

The Finnish flag is white and blue.
The wind blew the balloon away.

Lack of sleep does affect me.
It has a strong effect on my schoolwork.

Devon is already in eighth grade.
He is all ready for high school.

An ant crawled onto the picnic basket.
Roger's aunt is his dad's sister.

I walked by the restaurant.
I decided to buy a bite-sized burger.

Read the following story. If an underlined word is incorrect, cross it out and write the correct form above it. If the underlined word is correct, leave it alone. The first error has been corrected for you.

My ~~ant~~ aunt asked me, "Shane, would you go to the store to buy some milk?"

I said, "I think we ~~all ready~~ already have some milk."

She said, "I need more than the amount we have for this recipe."

She gave me some money, and I left the house. The sun was shining in a blue sky, so it was a nice day for a walk. As I crossed a rather busy street, my hat ~~blue~~ blew off. I wanted to chase after it, ~~accept~~ except there were cars coming from both directions. I returned to the sidewalk and waited for the traffic to clear.

At that moment, something happened that had a big affect [effect] on me. From among [between] two cars, a short-haired, black and white puppy darted out into the road. I knew I had to do something. I was all ready to run after the dog when the sound of screeching tires broke through the normal traffic noises.

My heart was ~~all ready~~ [already] pounding. I quickly scanned the scene, looking among all the cars that had stopped. Then I saw the puppy—on the street buy [by] two of the motionless cars. I ran to it and saw that it was crouching down, scared of all the commotion. What a relief! I scooped up the puppy. The ~~amount~~ [number] of people who had come to see what happened began to clap.

Then an older man ran up to me. "Oh, thank you, thank you," he said as he took the pup from me. He was clearly out of breath from running after the dog, which had slipped out of its collar. He put a collar and leash back on the dog, which happily sniffed some ants crawling ~~between~~ [among] all the cracks in the pavement.

"Please ~~except~~ [accept] this," he said as he reached into his pocket. "I am very grateful." He handed me a five-dollar bill. I tried to refuse, but he insisted.

When I returned home with the milk, I told ~~Ant~~ [Aunt] Irene about the adventure. She asked, "Does this ~~effect~~ [affect] your desire to get your own puppy?"

"No way," I replied. "But I *do* see how important a leash is!"

Next Step Use the following pairs or sets of words correctly in sentences (use one set of words per sentence): *fewer, less; altogether, all together;* and *it's, its.* Share your results.

Example:

"Visiting the capitol building is a capital idea," said Grandpa.
(The words "capitol" and "capital" are used correctly in this sentence.)

Using the Right Word 2

Learn the difference between some commonly misused words in this exercise. (See pages 662–666 in *Write Source* for this information.)

Examples

Do not **desert** a friend in need.	Japan is **farther** away than Mexico is.
We'll have brownies for **dessert**.	Ask the teacher for **further** information.
That was a **good** movie.	Lana wears **fewer** rings than I do.
Marva sings very **well**.	Each year there is **less** water in the pond.
Did you **hear** that sound?	The rabbit chewed a **hole** in the fence.
The mail is **here**.	I read the **whole** book in one day.

If the underlined word is incorrect, cross it out and write the correct form above it. Do not change a correct word. The first one has been done for you.

less
1. Rochelle wanted more trees and ~~fewer~~ grass in her yard.

here
2. "I could plant an apple tree ~~hear~~," she thought.

hole
3. She dug a deep, wide ~~whole~~ in the dirt.

4. She wanted to give the young tree a good start.

5. A little farther out in the yard, Rochelle planted a pear tree.

well
6. As time passed, both trees grew quite ~~good~~.

fewer
7. There were ~~less~~ pears than apples.

whole
8. Rochelle picked a ~~hole~~ bushel of red apples from the tree.

dessert
9. She made a ~~desert~~ with some of the apples.

whole
10. One of her neighbors said, "I have a ~~hole~~ book of recipes."

hear
11. "I ~~here~~ that one of the best is for applesauce," she added.

further
12. Rochelle needed ~~farther~~ help to pick the rest of the fruit.

Using the Right Word 3

Write Source explains all of the following commonly misused words. (See pages 668–674 in *Write Source* for this information.)

Examples

Please lay the flowers on the counter.
I am going to lie down.

Grandpa earned a medal in the war.
Platinum is a fine metal.

The past two years have been hard for me.
Ramón passed Ally on his bike.

It's raining.
The dog chased its tail.

Children learn manners at home.
Parents teach their children a lot.

Will we see peace in our lifetimes?
Whiskers ate a piece of tuna.

Cross out any underlined word that is incorrect and write the correct form above it. Do not change a word that is correct. The first sentence has been done for you.

1. Many people feel more at ~~piece~~ *peace* with a dog in the house.
2. ~~Its~~ *It's* too bad that my dog could not learn to roll over.
3. Mr. Evans has never ~~past~~ *passed* up a chance to work with a puppy.
4. He can ~~learn~~ *teach* any dog to sit, lie, stay, and come.
5. His ~~passed~~ *past* "students" have won ~~metals~~ *medals* at dog shows.
6. One dog can balance a ~~peace~~ *piece* of food on ~~it's~~ *its* nose.
7. Another will ~~lie~~ *lay* a ball right at your feet so that you will throw it.
8. Mr. Evans doesn't care for the collars with ~~medal~~ *metal* decorations.
9. Most dogs can learn to live at ~~piece~~ *peace* with cats.
10. In the ~~passed~~ *past*, ~~its~~ *it's* likely that cats and dogs were enemies.

Next Step Use the following pairs of words correctly in sentences (use one set of words per sentence): *its, it's; peace, piece;* and *learn, teach.* Share your results.

Using the Right Word 4

Write Source lists many of the words that are commonly misused in writing, including the following. (See pages 676–686 in *Write Source* for this information.)

Examples

The gymnasium floor is a real problem.
It really needs to be replaced.

Wearing glasses improves my sight.
Broken glass covers the site of the accident.

They're loading up their car for a trip.
When will they get there?

I wonder whose mittens these are.
She's the one who's drawing a dragon.

I love to sit and read on the sofa.
Frank set his books on the shelf.

Your little sister is adorable.
Did you say that you're leaving?

If an underlined word is incorrect, cross it out and write the correct form above it. Do not change a correct word. The first one has been done for you.

1. Kim and Lonnie forgot ~~they're~~ *their* lunches today, so ~~there~~ *they're* really hungry.
2. A man ~~who's~~ *whose* car was scratched at the construction site was angry.
3. Did anyone ever tell you that ~~your~~ *you're* a ~~real~~ *really* beautiful person?
4. Go ahead and ~~set~~ *sit* in one of the chairs ~~their~~ *there* in the waiting room.
5. Grandma Joan, ~~whose~~ *who's* losing her ~~site~~ *sight*, will have eye surgery soon.
6. After the exam, the teacher said, "Please ~~sit~~ *set* ~~you're~~ *your* pens and pencils down."
7. Mickey and Edwina said that ~~their~~ *they're* looking for a real gold nugget.
8. ~~Whose~~ *Who's* staying at ~~you're~~ *your* house tonight?
9. ~~Their~~ *There* is a ~~real~~ *really* great ~~sight~~ *site* for a skate park downtown.

Using the Right Word Review 1

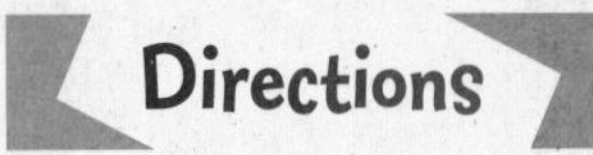

In the following story, draw a line through any word used incorrectly and write the correct form above it. The first one has been corrected for you. (See pages 652–686 in *Write Source*.)

When our neighbor's cocker spaniel had puppies, I got the pick of the ~~hole~~ *whole* litter. I had to choose from ~~among~~ *between* two blond pups. The one I chose had little white paws and freckles. I named him Snooze because ~~their~~ *there* was no puppy that liked sleeping as much as he did. I didn't know much about puppies, but I had time to learn.

My dad and I had to ~~by~~ *buy* wood to build a doghouse. Then my mom said she'd ~~learn~~ *teach* me how to train my dog to do tricks. We went to the library and borrowed a number of books about dog obedience. We read about house-training a dog with compliments (not punishment) and about ~~learning~~ *teaching* it to stay and ~~set~~ *sit*. Every morning I'd visit Snooze at my neighbor's house. He would ~~here~~ *hear* me coming and wag his tail ~~real~~ *really* wildly. We ~~past~~ *passed* the time getting to know each other. By the time Snooze came home, he ~~all ready~~ *already* knew how to heel and give me his paw to shake.

Snooze is smarter than any other dog I know. He has an ~~effect~~ *affect* on everyone in the house. ~~Accept~~ *Except* for all the blond hair he leaves when he ~~lays~~ *lies* on all the furniture, he is a ~~well~~ *good* dog. ~~Its~~ *It's* hard to imagine life without Snooze after these ~~passed~~ *past* few months.

Next Step Use the following pairs of words correctly in sentences (use one set of words per sentence): *who's, whose; past, passed;* and *good, well.* Share your results.

Using the Right Word Review 2

In the following story, draw a line through any word used incorrectly and write the correct form above it. The first one has been corrected for you. (See pages 652–686 in *Write Source*.)

Whether ~~your~~ *you're* a dog lover or a cat lover, you'll like this brief history of cats. While cats were running wild through the African jungles, dogs had ~~all ready~~ *already* moved in with humans. An unknown Egyptian tamed an African wild cat, and in no time at all, cats were ~~real~~ *really* popular in ancient Egypt.

With the cats around, there were ~~less~~ *fewer* rats. The Egyptians were grateful. In fact, the cats did their job so ~~good~~ *well* that they were soon worshiped as gods. Of course, as anyone ~~whose~~ *who's* ever owned a cat knows, this suited the cats just fine. They always act like ~~there~~ *they're* the center of attention.

Did you know that when a cat ~~past~~ *passed* away in ancient Egypt, you had to show ~~you're~~ *your* grief by shaving off your eyebrows? And whoever killed a cat (even accidentally) was subject to ~~farther~~ *further* punishment. (These Egyptians were really serious about ~~they're~~ *their* precious cats!) A law was ~~past~~ *passed* so no one could take cats out of Egypt. However, sailors began to smuggle them out, and people around the Mediterranean would ~~by~~ *buy* them. The cats had quite an ~~affect~~ *effect* on Europeans, and their pets were well loved.

Given this history, is it any wonder that you can't ~~learn~~ *teach* a cat to ~~set~~ *sit* down or ~~lie~~ *lay* its head on your lap . . . unless it wants to? It would be an insult to ~~it's~~ *its* heritage!

Directions Use the following pairs or sets of words correctly in sentences. (Use two words in a single sentence, or write a separate sentence for each one.)

1. affect, effect

2. learn, teach

3. your, you're

4. accept, except

5. fewer, less

6. their, they're, there

Sentence Activities

The activities in this section cover three important areas: (1) the basic parts of sentences, (2) common sentence errors, and (3) ways to add variety to sentences. Most activities include a main practice part in which you review, combine, or analyze different sentences. In addition, the **Next Step** activities give you follow-up practice with certain skills.

Sentence Basics	**63**
Sentence Problems	**75**
Sentence Variety	**91**

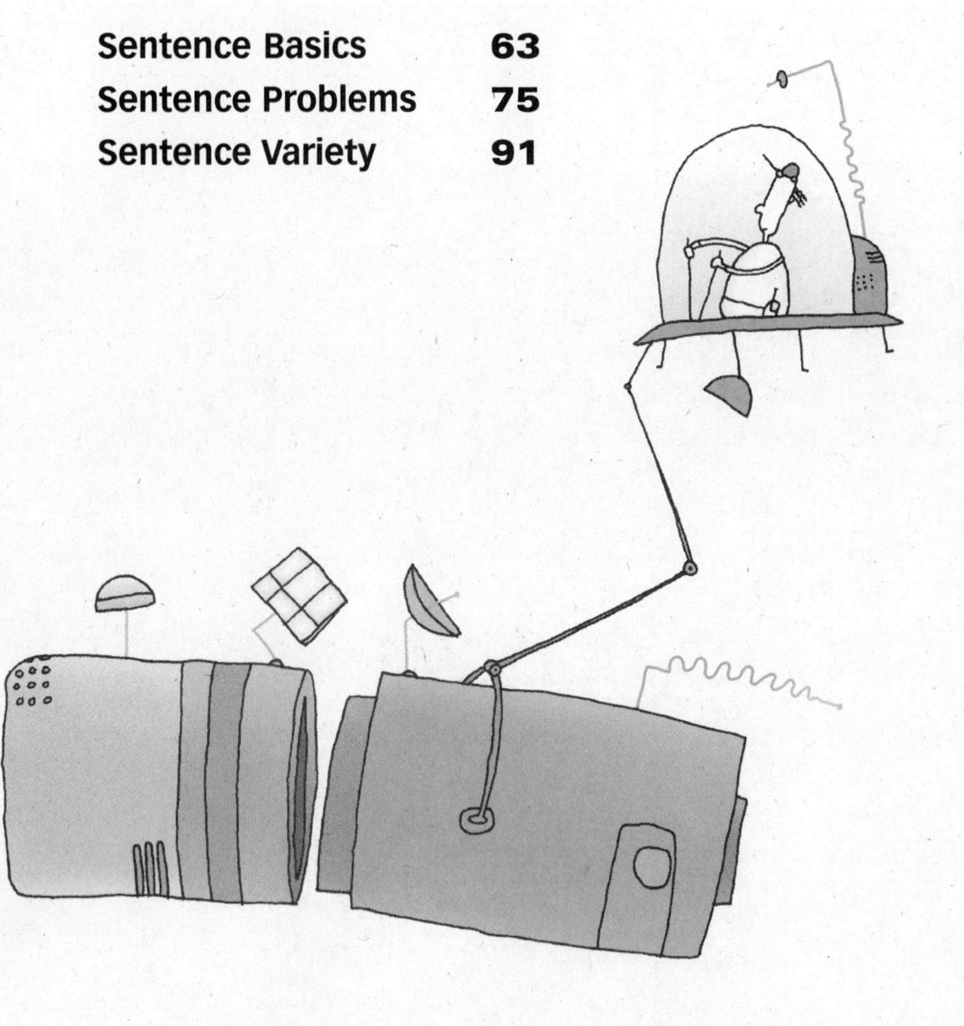

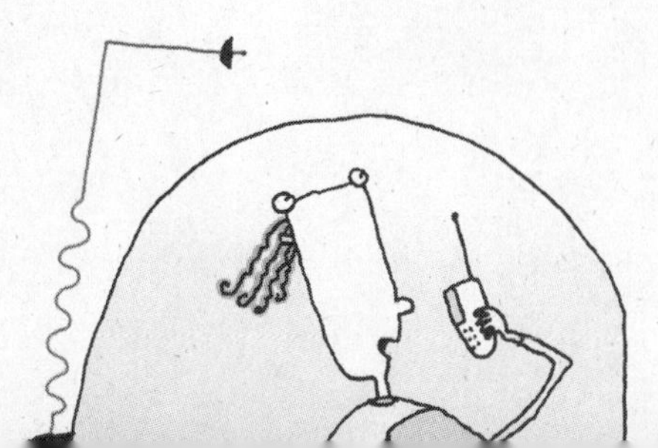

Subjects and Predicates 1

All sentences must have a subject and a predicate (verb) to express a complete thought. The subject is the part of a sentence that is doing something or is being talked about. The **simple subject** is the subject without its modifiers. The predicate is the part of the sentence that says something about the subject or tells what the subject is doing. The **simple predicate** is the predicate (verb) without the words that describe or modify it. (See 690.2 and 692.2 in *Write Source*.)

Examples

Simple Subject:
The ancient Romans counted their citizens regularly.

Simple Predicate:
The ancient Romans counted their citizens regularly.

In the sentences that follow, underline the simple subject once and the simple predicate twice. *Note:* Helping verbs (*can, could, should, may, have, had,* and so on) are part of the simple predicate. (See 718.3 in *Write Source* for a list of the most common helping verbs.) The first one has been done for you.

1. The U.S. government conducts a census every 10 years.
2. A census is a survey that counts people by age, gender, occupation, and so on.
3. Different surveys collect different types of information.
4. The United States gathers more census information than any other country.
5. No census information can get anyone into trouble with the law.
6. In ancient times, the local folk disliked any census.

7. Higher taxes were often the result of a Roman census.

8. The ancient Babylonians collected census information on clay tablets.

9. Fewer than 4 million people lived in the United States at the time of the first census.

10. In 1790, most people lived in 16 states in the eastern part of the United States.

11. Census information determines the number of representatives of each state to the U.S. House of Representatives.

12. In addition, the census gives federal, state, and local governments important information for future planning.

13. Businesses use the census information for their planning as well.

Next Step Suppose you were asked to conduct a survey in your school about athletics, television, or reading habits. With the help of a classmate, write five questions for your survey. Then survey a group of students and compile your results.

Subjects and Predicates 2

All sentences must have a subject and a predicate to express a complete thought. (See 690.1–690.3 and 692.1–692.3 in *Write Source* for more information.) In the example sentences, the simple subject is underlined once, and the simple predicate is underlined twice.

Examples

Lasers have hundreds of uses.

Laser light is much brighter than sunlight.

Directions **In the following sentences, underline the simple subject with one line and the simple predicate with two lines. The first sentence has been done for you.**

1. In some cases, laser beams are red.
2. Light from a laser travels in a narrow line, or beam.
3. In contrast, electric light spreads out into a wide beam.
4. Doctors use lasers in many kinds of surgery.
5. Lasers record music onto compact discs.
6. Lasers in CD players then play the music.
7. In stores, lasers read price tags.
8. Laser beams carry television pictures and telephone conversations.
9. Diamonds are extremely hard.
10. Lasers easily drill holes in diamonds.

Directions In each sentence below, underline the simple subject with one line and the simple predicate with two lines. The first sentence has been done for you.

1. Often, inventions have very interesting beginnings.
2. The Frisbee began as a pie pan.
3. College students bought some pies at Frisbie Bakery in Connecticut.
4. They ate the pies, of course.
5. Then they played catch with the empty pie pans.
6. The name of the bakery was on the pans.
7. With each toss, the students yelled, "Frisbie!"
8. The game spread to other colleges.
9. A company in California made the first Frisbee.
10. It flew better than a pie pan.
11. In time, people invented many different Frisbee games.
12. Before long, dogs joined in, too.

Next Step Write two sentences about Frisbee disks. Then underline the simple subjects with one line and the simple predicates with two lines.

Compound Subjects and Predicates

A sentence may have a compound subject, a compound predicate, or both. See the examples below. The compound subjects are underlined with one line, and the compound predicates are underlined with two lines. (See 690.4 and 692.6 in *Write Source* or more information.)

Examples

Jason and Mason play in the Intergalactic Football League.
(The subject "Jason" and "Mason" is compound.)

Mason plays linebacker and returns punts.
(The predicate "plays" and "returns" is compound.)

Jason and Mason block and tackle for a living.
(The subject and predicate are both compound.)

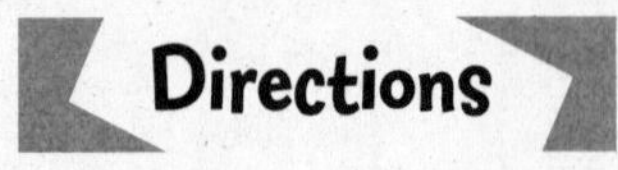

Underline each simple subject with one line and each simple predicate with two lines. In each sentence, the subject or predicate may or may not be compound. The first sentence has been done for you.

1. Jim came in and sat down.
2. Molly and I watched a video.
3. Jonathan logged on and checked his e-mail.
4. He got an e-mail from his cousins in Tokyo.
5. Andrew and Hannah wrote about life in Japan.
6. They still play baseball and go to movies.
7. They ride a train, instead of a bus, to school.
8. Hannah reads and writes Japanese.

Directions **All of the following sentences have a compound subject, a compound predicate, or both. Underline each simple subject with one line and each simple predicate with two lines. The first sentence has been done for you.**

1. Slick roads or heavy traffic sometimes makes us late for school.
2. The teacher went to the board and started writing.
3. Our neighbors went to the Grand Canyon and hiked for a week.
4. They took pictures and brought back postcards.
5. Shannon and I heard all about their trip.
6. After dinner, Ross and Lindsey do their homework and play computer games.
7. Summer and fall are my favorite times of year.
8. Snow or ice on the roads slows traffic and makes driving dangerous.
9. Earth orbits the sun and rotates on its axis.
10. Neptune and Pluto are farther from the sun and colder than Earth.
11. Tim wrote a science-fiction story and put it on our Web site.
12. Some students in Australia saw his story and liked it.

Next Step Write three sentences that have both a compound subject and a compound predicate. Underline the compound subjects with one line and the compound predicates with two lines.

Clauses

A clause is a group of words containing a subject and a predicate. An **independent clause** presents a complete thought and can stand alone as a sentence. A **dependent clause** does not present a complete thought and cannot stand alone. A dependent clause must be connected to an independent clause. (See page 698.)

A dependent clause begins with a subordinating conjunction—*after, although, because, before, when, while,* and so on—or a relative pronoun—*who, whom, whose, which, that,* and so on. (See 710.1 and 744.2 in *Write Source* for additional examples of both types of words.)

Note: A sentence containing an independent clause and a dependent clause is called a complex sentence. (See page 746 in *Write Source* for more information.)

Examples

Although I don't like writing letters, I love getting them.
("Although I don't like writing letters" is a dependent clause beginning with a subordinating conjunction. "I love getting them" is an independent clause.)

I really enjoy letters that include funny stories.
("I really enjoy letters" is an independent clause. "That include funny stories" is a dependent clause beginning with a relative pronoun.)

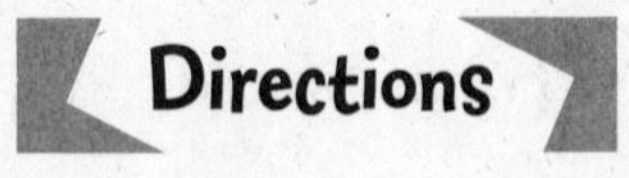

Read the following sentences. Underline each independent clause. Put parentheses ( ) around each dependent clause. The first sentence has been done for you. (One sentence has two dependent clauses.)

1. (Although I always appreciate gifts), I find it hard to write formal thank-you letters.
2. It is especially hard (when my mother is on my case).
3. (Because this is such a big deal with my mother), I'm trying to understand the issues.
4. My mother is someone (who is very set in her ways).
5. (If only she counted telephone calls and e-mail), I would be off the hook.

6. (As soon as I open a gift), I like to call the person and say thank you.

7. Formal thank-you notes sound phony to me, (while a phone call or an e-mail message seems much more natural).

8. My mother insists on a handwritten thank-you (because that is what she has always done).

9. What is so special about writing by hand (when there are other ways of accomplishing the same thing)?

10. Why do we have telephones and computers (if we aren't allowed to use them for everyday things)?

11. (If a person has e-mail), I have no trouble getting on the computer and keying in a note of thanks.

12. I enjoy technology (that allows me to work quickly and efficiently).

13. (Even though my birthday was two weeks ago), I still haven't gotten around to writing my thank-you note to Uncle Bert.

14. (If I would send him an e-mail message), I have no idea (what would happen with my mom).

Next Step Write a friendly letter or a thank-you note to someone who deserves to hear from you. Actually send the letter, and experience the good feeling you get from corresponding with someone. Turn to *Write Source* for guidelines and models.

Prepositional Phrases

A phrase is a group of words that is missing a subject, a predicate, or both. In most cases, a phrase works as a modifier in a sentence. The most common type of phrase is the prepositional phrase. Every prepositional phrase begins with a preposition (*in, at, by, with,* and so on) and ends with the object of the preposition (the nearest noun or pronoun). In between may be words that modify the object of the preposition. (Study the examples below and then see 742.1 in *Write Source* for more information.)

Examples

Stephanie plays basketball in her driveway.
(preposition: "in"; object: "driveway"; modifier: "her")

The ball belongs to Stephanie and me.
(preposition: "to"; compound object: "Stephanie" and "me")

Underline the prepositional phrases in the sentences that follow. Circle each preposition. Draw an arrow to each object of a preposition. The first sentence has been done for you. (The number of prepositional phrases is listed in parentheses after each sentence.)

1. How much do you know about the game of basketball? *(2)*
2. The game of basketball was invented by Dr. James Naismith in 1891 for indoor use in a YMCA program. *(5)*
3. For his first game, Naismith used a soccer ball and two peach baskets for goals. *(2)*
4. Soon basketball was played throughout the United States. *(1)*
5. Before the modern baskets, net bags were attached to the hoops. *(2)*
6. Today, millions of fans crowd into arenas for professional games. *(3)*

7. Each team has five players on the floor. *(1)*

8. The leader of the team on the court is usually the point guard—a quick player with good ball-handling skills. *(3)*

9. The team also has two forwards; they are taller than the guards and play in the area from the end line to the free throw lane. *(3)*

10. The tallest player on the team is the center with many important duties, including shot-blocking and rebounding. *(2)*

11. Basketball is now played in 200 countries worldwide by men and women of all ages. *(3)*

12. The beauty of basketball is that it can be played in a fancy gym, in a driveway, or on a small city playground. *(4)*

13. For the fun and excitement of the game, we say, "Thanks, Dr. Naismith, and hip, hip, hooray for basketball!" *(3)*

Next Step Write a paragraph about one of your memorable (or not so memorable) basketball experiences, either as a player or as a spectator. Underline any prepositional phrases you use. Share your results.

Transitions

The effective use of transitions can help you achieve effective organization and smooth-reading sentences in your writing. Transitions are words such as *first, second, soon, finally,* and so on. (See pages 572–573 in *Write Source* for a list of transitions.)

Use the following transition words to complete the story that follows. Try to use each transition only once. The first one has been done for you.

and	**for example**	**then**
before	**for this reason**	**third**
besides	**however**	**throughout**
but	**in addition**	**today**
finally	**on the other hand**	**to repeat**
first	**second**	

Nobody knows when the first dog became a regular at some cave dweller's fire circle. ____However____, we do know that dogs were the first domesticated animals. ____Throughout____ recorded history, dogs and people have been buddies. Some dogs have even been considered sacred. ____For example____, one Native American myth says that even the Creator of the universe was accompanied by a dog. ____Today____, in this country, the American Kennel Club recognizes 150 different breeds of dogs. On the one hand, you might choose a miniature Chihuahua who weighs under two pounds. ____On the other hand____, you may prefer a large breed such as a St. Bernard that tips the scales at 200 pounds.

___Before___ a dog can do its best, it must be treated kindly and be trained well. ___Then___ it will try hard to please and to serve. ___For this reason___, a well-trained dog has many career opportunities. ___First___, there are jobs in agriculture. ___In addition___ to herding cattle and sheep, dogs cheerfully pull sleds, retrieve objects, hunt, and perform other chores. ___Second___, there are jobs in law enforcement. ___Besides___ being natural guardians of their territory and their friends, dogs have an incredible sense of smell that can detect a drop of blood in five quarts of water—a handy skill in this line of work. ___Third___, there are opportunities for dogs in the social services. Of course, dogs can be trained to help people who are blind to cross streets safely, ___but___ they can also pick up objects for people in wheelchairs and cheer up people who are depressed. ___Finally___, dogs are natural athletes and entertainers. The circus ___and___ the TV and movie industry are always looking for a few good dogs to join their ranks. ___To repeat___, dogs have many career opportunities, but I'm just happy my dog isn't particularly ambitious.

Next Step Explain a simple process (teaching a dog a new trick, fixing something, cooking, and so on) in a few sentences. Use transitions such as *first, second, for example,* and *finally* in your explanation.

Sentence Fragments

A sentence must have a subject and a predicate, and it must also express a complete thought. A **fragment** occurs when a group of words is missing either a subject or a verb, or it doesn't express a complete thought. At first glance, a sentence fragment may look like an acceptable sentence because it starts with a capital letter and ends with a period (or other end punctuation mark). (See pages 504–505 in *Write Source*.)

Examples

Sentence Fragment:	*Complete Sentence:*
In less than 10 hours.	**Jupiter rotates in less than 10 hours.** (A subject and a verb have been added.)
Has 58 moons.	**Jupiter has 58 moons.** (A subject has been added.)
Jupiter's diameter 11 times bigger than Earth's.	**Jupiter's diameter is 11 times bigger than Earth's.** (A verb has been added.)

Write an "F" on the line before each group of words that is a sentence fragment and an "S" before each complete sentence. On your own paper, change the fragments into complete sentences.

S 1. Jupiter is the largest planet.

F 2. Is the fifth planet from the sun.

F 3. Jupiter, made of gas and some rock, a huge, red globe.

F 4. Jupiter so large that 1,300 Earths could fit inside it.

S 5. Jupiter gives off more heat than it receives.

F 6. Is about as big as it can be.

F 7. This ball of hydrogen and helium, fifth brightest object in the sky.

F 8. Has one main ring.

S 9. Jupiter was named after the Roman king of the gods.

Directions Write an "F" on the line before each group of words that is a sentence fragment and an "S" before each complete sentence. On your own paper, change the fragments into complete sentences.

F 1. My favorite kind of TV show.

S 2. I don't have time for television on school nights.

S 3. Story settings in faraway places fascinate me.

F 4. Starships, space missions, and alien races.

S 5. The odd creature was one of the first aliens encountered by the space exploration team.

F 6. Able to compute numbers and call up information.

F 7. Keeps me on the edge of my seat with mystery and suspense.

S 8. Isn't it interesting to think about life in the twenty-second century?

F 9. Despite exploring the galaxy and expanding intelligence.

S 10. A good sci-fi fantasy on TV helps me "space out."

F 11. May be the way you feel, too.

Next Step Suppose a friend calls to tell you an amazing story, but because of noise, you pick up only fragments of the conversation. On your own paper, turn the fragments below into complete sentences that form a story. Compare stories made out of these fragments.

looked out my window . . .
heard strange noises and . . .
exploring we saw . . .
think it was . . .

Run-Ons 1

One form of run-on sentence is a **comma splice**. It occurs in writing when two simple sentences are incorrectly joined with a comma. A comma plus a connecting word, an end punctuation mark, or a semicolon should be used between two simple sentences. Another form of **run-on sentence** occurs when two simple sentences are incorrectly joined without punctuation or a connecting word. (See page 506 in *Write Source* for examples.)

Directions

In the groups of words below, place a "CS" in front of each comma splice, an "RO" in front of each run-on sentence, and a "C" in front of each correct sentence. Correct the sentence errors. The first two have been done for you.

RO 1. Mars is the fourth planet from the sun. It is the one you can see most clearly from Earth.

C 2. Mars is only one-half the size of Earth.

CS 3. Mars shines with red and orange light, and it is often called the Red Planet.

RO 4. The Romans named Mars after their god of war because its red color reminded them of blood and war.

RO 5. Mars has seasons like those on Earth. Its days are also about 24 hours long.

C 6. Mars has two moons called Phobos and Deimos.

CS 7. People used to believe that there were people on Mars, and they made up stories about Martians.

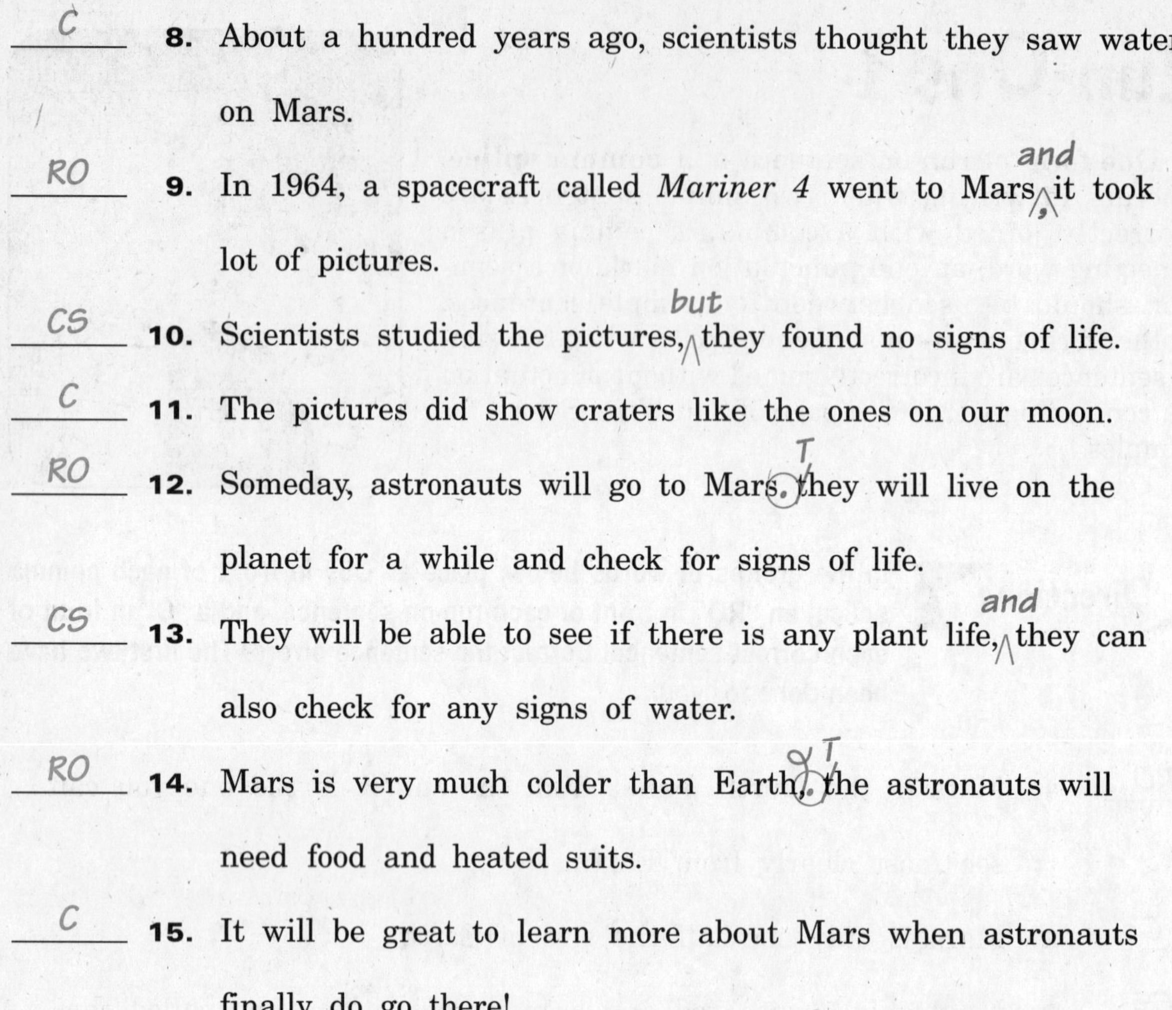

C 8. About a hundred years ago, scientists thought they saw water on Mars.

RO 9. In 1964, a spacecraft called *Mariner 4* went to Mars, and it took a lot of pictures.

CS 10. Scientists studied the pictures, but they found no signs of life.

C 11. The pictures did show craters like the ones on our moon.

RO 12. Someday, astronauts will go to Mars. They will live on the planet for a while and check for signs of life.

CS 13. They will be able to see if there is any plant life, and they can also check for any signs of water.

RO 14. Mars is very much colder than Earth. The astronauts will need food and heated suits.

C 15. It will be great to learn more about Mars when astronauts finally do go there!

Next Step Let's say you want to know more about Mars and other planets in our solar system. Certainly you could refer to a book about the planets in your school library. You could also turn to an encyclopedia, your science textbook, or the Internet. Write down two facts you learn about the planet.

Run-Ons 2

To become a good writer, you need to learn as much as you can about sentences. You need to read plenty of other writers' sentences, you need to practice writing your own sentences, and you need to acquire a working knowledge of the sentence basics—including a clear understanding of the different types of sentence errors.

Directions **Put an "RO" in front of any run-on sentences that follow, a "CS" in front of any comma splices, and an "C" in front of any complete sentences. (See page 506 in *Write Source* for examples and information about these sentence errors.)**

RO **1.** Gwendolyn Brooks loves people you can tell that the first time you meet her.

CS **2.** I heard her read her poetry in a Chicago bookstore, she drew a big crowd.

RO **3.** We had all come to see and hear the famous poet read some of her poetry I felt like I was in the presence of a living legend.

CS **4.** I love her poem "We Real Cool," this is a poem about kids playing pool.

C **5.** When Ms. Brooks was reading her poems, she made eye contact with each of us.

CS **6.** She looked like she could be anybody's favorite aunt, that day she wore a navy blue suit and sensible shoes and carried a big black handbag.

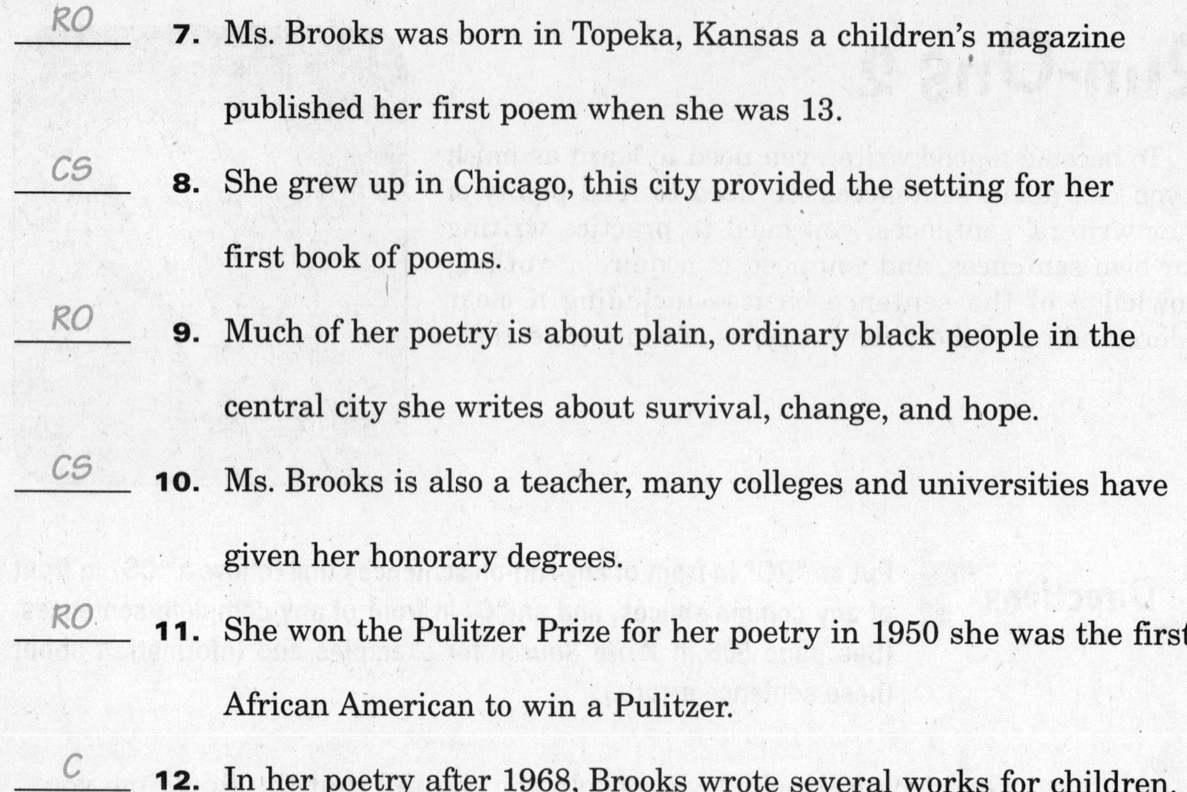

RO 7. Ms. Brooks was born in Topeka, Kansas a children's magazine published her first poem when she was 13.

CS 8. She grew up in Chicago, this city provided the setting for her first book of poems.

RO 9. Much of her poetry is about plain, ordinary black people in the central city she writes about survival, change, and hope.

CS 10. Ms. Brooks is also a teacher, many colleges and universities have given her honorary degrees.

RO 11. She won the Pulitzer Prize for her poetry in 1950 she was the first African American to win a Pulitzer.

C 12. In her poetry after 1968, Brooks wrote several works for children.

Next Step Review "Writing Other Forms of Poetry" on page 359 in *Write Source*. Then write a limerick, name poem, or phrase poem about success.

Sentence Problems Review 1

Run-on sentences, comma splices, and sentence fragments are three of the most common types of sentence errors. One of your most important jobs when you edit is to check your writing for these types of errors. If your sentences aren't clear and correct, readers will have a hard time following your ideas. *Remember:* Accurate copy is one of the traits of good writing. (To review each of these types of sentence errors, see pages 504–506 in *Write Source*.)

Write "RO" in front of any run-on sentences, "CS" in front of any comma splices, and "F" in front of any fragments. The first sentence has been done for you.

CS 1. "Down under" refers to countries that are south of the equator, however, we usually just think of Australia and New Zealand.

CS 2. In Australia, January and February are the warmest months, June and July are the coldest ones.

RO 3. Australia is the world's smallest continent it is also the sixth-largest country.

F 4. Much of its interior dry and hot.

RO 5. About 70 percent of its birds and 90 percent of its snakes are unique to Australia they cannot be found anywhere else in the world.

CS 6. Australia is famous for its unusual wildlife, kangaroos, koalas, and wombats are only three of its strange animals.

CS 7. The original people of Australia are called Aborigines, they came to Australia from Southeast Asia about 40,000 years ago.

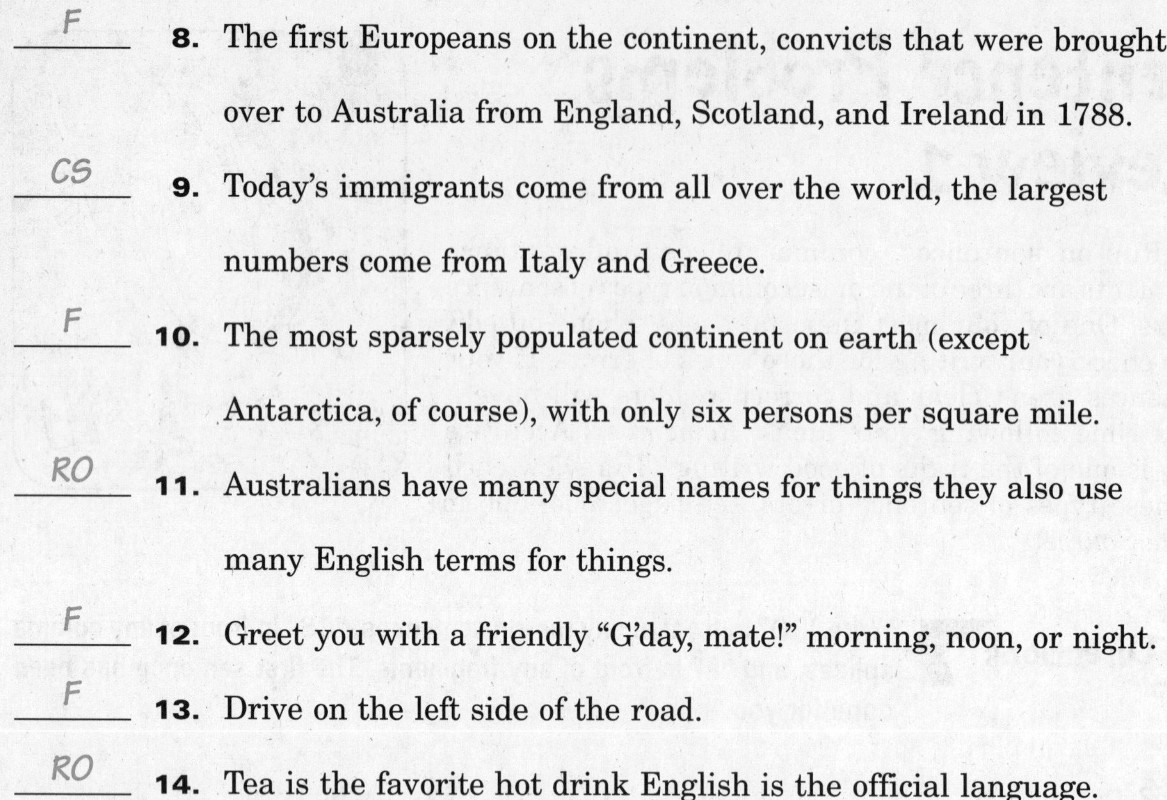

F 8. The first Europeans on the continent, convicts that were brought over to Australia from England, Scotland, and Ireland in 1788.

CS 9. Today's immigrants come from all over the world, the largest numbers come from Italy and Greece.

F 10. The most sparsely populated continent on earth (except Antarctica, of course), with only six persons per square mile.

RO 11. Australians have many special names for things they also use many English terms for things.

F 12. Greet you with a friendly "G'day, mate!" morning, noon, or night.

F 13. Drive on the left side of the road.

RO 14. Tea is the favorite hot drink English is the official language.

Next Step Study a map of Australia. What is its capital? What seas surround Australia? What are its latitude and longitude? What are the names of two of its great deserts? Approximately how far is it from Hawaii? Gather these facts and combine them into several complete sentences that give the basic geographic facts about the continent that is "down under."

Sentence Problems Review 2

Sentences have a way of running out of control. Your goal as a writer should be to avoid the errors that lead to "wayword" sentences. Three of the most common types of sentence errors are run-on sentences, comma splices, and sentence fragments. (See pages 504–506 in *Write Source* for explanations and examples.)

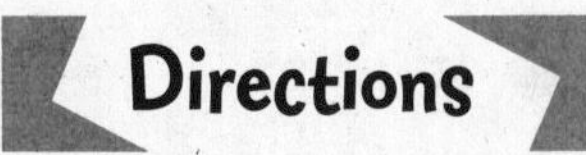

Write "RO" in front of any run-on sentences that follow, "CS" in front of any comma splices, and "F" in front of any sentence fragments.

RO **1.** Yesterday, Indra and I hiked into the woods we wanted to have a picnic lunch with a nice crowd of trees.

F **2.** Some sandwiches, chips, and pop in a backpack.

CS **3.** We had to hike 2 1/2 miles to get to shade, the shortest trail in the park was 4 miles.

CS **4.** It was hot on that trail, we were sweaty, cranky, and red faced.

CS **5.** Our pop got warm, the sandwiches wilted.

RO **6.** The woods were raining wood ticks they fell on our hair and climbed inside our clothes.

F **7.** Picked ticks out of my hair when we rested.

F **8.** Totally grossed me out!

CS **9.** The ants drove me crazy, Indra called me a wimp.

F **10.** Until she got stung by a bee.

Next Step Rewrite this little story in complete sentences on your own paper. What else might have happened on this outing? Add your ideas to continue the story. Make sure to use complete sentences. Share your results.

Rambling Sentences

Be careful not to use too many *and*'s, *but*'s, and *so*'s in your own writing. Otherwise, your sentences might ramble on like those of an excited four-year-old. (Turn to "Eliminate Rambling Sentences" on page 507 in *Write Source* for more information and an example.)

Directions **Read the following paragraph aloud. Listen for sentences that seem to go on forever. Correct these sentences by taking out some (but not all) of the *and*'s, *but*'s, and *so*'s. Then fix the punctuation and capitalization as needed. The first few rambling ideas have been corrected for you.**

We went up to my grandfather's cabin last weekend. It was fantastic. We went fishing on Saturday morning, and I caught a bass off the pier, so Dad said he'd have Mom cook the fish for lunch. Cleaning a fish is kind of gross because you have to cut it open, but Dad did most of that, and then we went swimming in the lake. My brother Tad and I took turns pushing each other out over the water in a tire swing. Tad would push me hard, and I'd jump off into the water, and then he'd yell for me to swim back and push him, and we spent all afternoon swimming and pushing. On Sunday morning, Dad cooked pancakes and thick, crunchy bacon on the old wood-burning stove, and we ate like pigs, and Tad and I wanted to go swimming again, but then we decided to go for a hike instead. We looked for creepy bugs while we were in the woods and we found slugs, centipedes, and caterpillars, but we also caught a few butterflies, but we let them go. We kept a couple of the caterpillars in a jar and looked at them all the way home in the car.

Subject-Verb Agreement 1

Here are some definite signs of agreement: a nod of the head, a handshake, and a signature on a contract. Do you know of any others? Here's one that has to do with writing and speaking. A singular subject *(my friend)* used with a singular verb *(listens)* is a definite sign of agreement. In the same way, a plural subject *(my friends)* used with a plural verb *(listen)* is another sign of agreement.

Subjects and verbs used together must agree in number. That is, they must both be singular or plural. Study the examples below to see what we mean. (See pages 508–509 in *Write Source* for more information.)

Examples

My friends go with me every year to the state fair.

(Both the subject and verb are plural, so they agree.)

Carlos and I ride the rocket cars.

(Compound subjects connected by "and" require plural verbs. "Ride" is plural.)

Everyone enjoys the music in the grandstand area.

(Indefinite pronouns like "everyone" require singular verbs. "Enjoys" is a singular verb, so the subject and verb agree.)

Neither Alfredo nor Jim likes amusement rides.

(With compound subjects connected by "or" or "nor," the verb must agree with the subject nearest the verb. "Jim" is singular, so "likes" is singular.)

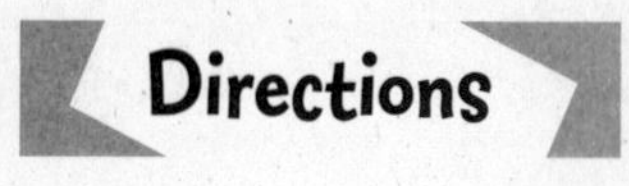

Directions

In each sentence, the subject is underlined with one line and the verb with two lines. Put a check next to each sentence in which the subject and verb do not agree. For those sentences you check, correct the subject-verb agreement errors. The first sentence has been done for you.

✔ **1.** At the fair, the parade of draft horses ~~are~~ *is* going to be on Sunday.

_____ **2.** One of my friends goes immediately to see the sideshows.

✔ 3. Cotton candy and caramel corn ~~is~~ are my favorite snacks.

✔ 4. Carlos and I ~~saves~~ save our money for the rides.

✔ 5. Jeremy and Zach ~~tries~~ try to win goldfish and stuffed animals.

_____ 6. The double Ferris wheel or the parachute drop is my favorite ride.

✔ 7. John, as well as my other friends, ~~love~~ loves the bumper cars.

_____ 8. My sister and Mary always go on the Tilt-A-Whirl ride.

✔ 9. A water ride or a roller coaster ~~are~~ is the coolest ride on a hot day.

✔ 10. Neither Julie nor Sally ~~visit~~ visits the animal barns.

_____ 11. Everybody likes to watch the pig races.

_____ 12. The pigs run much faster than you would think.

✔ 13. One of the pigs ~~run~~ runs professionally.

✔ 14. We all ~~loves~~ love the fair more than any other summertime activity.

Next Step Use your own paper to write about a time when you *disagreed* with a friend, a brother or sister, a teacher, or someone else about something. Don't forget that subjects and verbs must agree in all types of writing—even when you are writing about "disagreeable" topics. Share your results.

Subject-Verb Agreement 2

In order to check for subject-verb agreement, you must first identify the main subject and its verb. Underlining the main subject once and the verb twice in your rough drafts will help you look for subject-verb agreement in your own writing. (See pages 508 and 509 in *Write Source* for help with special kinds of agreement problems.)

Proofread the following passage. Underline the main subjects once and the verbs twice. Then check for subject-verb agreement problems. When you find an error, cross it out and write the correct word above it. The first sentence has been done for you. (If a sentence is correct, don't change it.)

A triathlon, with its combination of swimming, bicycling, and running, ~~are~~ *is* one of the most challenging sports events. The Ironman Triathlon, in Oahu, Hawaii, ~~have~~ *has* become the ultimate sports challenge among super athletes from all over the world. Of course, Hawaii's picture-perfect scenery and ideal climate probably ~~doesn't~~ *don't* hurt attendance any. A triathlon consists of the following events. First, each competitor swims 2.4 miles in the sea. After that, they all ~~bikes~~ *bike* for 112 miles. To top it off, all competitors ~~runs~~ *run* a 28-mile marathon. Yes, most of the competitors actually cross the finish line.

My two aunts, Helga and Sue, ~~has~~ have been training for a minitriathlon. Shorter distances ~~makes~~ make a minitriathlon more tolerable for an average, well-trained athlete. Neither of my aunts has competed in a triathlon before this year. Some in my family ~~calls~~ call Helga and Sue crazy. Those people probably ~~feels~~ feel jealous of my aunts. I, as well as most of my friends, admire my aunts' determination. Each of them ~~are~~ is doing the triathlon for personal reasons. In my book, they ~~is~~ are very cool.

Next Step Write several sentences about how you think you would do in a triathlon. Then have a classmate check your writing for subject-verb agreement.

Subject-Verb Agreement Review

Turn to pages 508 and 509 in *Write Source* to review the explanations and examples of some tricky subject-verb agreement problems.

Directions **On the blank at the beginning of each sentence, write the correct verb choice from the pair in parentheses. The first one has been done for you.**

1. ___has___ Someone just like you *(has, have)* invented every human-made object in the world.
2. ___was___ One of the tastiest inventions *(was, were)* created by accident.
3. ___are___ Imagine this scene. A certain Lord Montagu and his friends *(is, are)* enjoying a friendly game of cards 200 years ago in merry old England.
4. ___wants___ In the middle of a particularly intense round of cards, nobody *(want, wants)* to stop for lunch.
5. ___ring___ Either Lord Montagu or his friends *(ring, rings)* for a servant to bring food to the table.
6. ___brings___ The servant, in a well-ironed, black-and-white uniform, *(bring, brings)* in a tray of bread and meat.
7. ___lay___ On the table *(lay, lays)* the cards, one piled on top of the other.

8. ___pops___ Suddenly, into Lord Montagu's head, *(pop, pops)* the bright idea of stacking the bread and meat in a similar way.

9. ___is___ Everyone around the table *(is, are)* delighted.

10. ___find___ Most of the group *(find, finds)* they can eat and play cards at the same time.

11. ___travels___ News of the exciting invention *(travel, travels)* quickly.

12. ___becomes___ The whole concoction *(become, becomes)* known as a *sandwich* in honor of Lord Montagu, the fourth earl of Sandwich.

Next Step New inventions come from people who are looking for a better (faster, easier, cheaper) way of doing something. Create a new product or modify an old product with new ideas. Describe your invention in a few short sentences and share your writing with your classmates.

Combining Sentences Using Key Words

When you combine sentences, you make one smoother, more detailed sentence out of two or more short, choppy ones. One basic way to combine shorter sentences is to move a *key word* from one sentence to the other sentence. (See page 512 in *Write Source* for this information.)

Examples

Shorter Sentences:
Clyde's sister eats constantly. Clyde's sister is hungry.

Combined Sentence Using an Adjective:
Clyde's hungry sister eats constantly.

Shorter Sentences:
My mom loves coffee in the morning. She grinds it fresh.

Combined Sentence Using a Compound Adjective:
My mom loves fresh-ground coffee in the morning.

Shorter Sentences:
Tasha's dog begs for food at dinner. Tasha's dog slobbers.

Combined Sentence Using a Participle:
Tasha's slobbering dog begs for food at dinner.

Shorter Sentences:
I plan to go on a diet. I will go on the diet tomorrow.

Combined Sentence Using an Adverb:
Tomorrow I plan to go on a diet.

Combine the following sets of short sentences into longer ones, using the types of key words asked for in parentheses. Underline each key word you use. The first one has been done.

1. The wolves circled the dark cabin. The wolves were howling. **(participle)**

   The howling wolves circled the dark cabin.

2. Aunt Mae made liver and onions for dinner. She cooked dinner yesterday. **(adverb)**

Aunt Mae made liver and onions for dinner yesterday.

3. I like dogs. I like them when they are small. **(adjective)**

I like small dogs.

4. During the emergency, we dialed 911. We dialed quickly. **(adverb)**

During the emergency, we quickly dialed 911.

5. My shoes hurt my feet. My shoes are new. **(adjective)**

My new shoes hurt my feet.

6. The baseball fan received the last ticket. The baseball fan was smiling. **(participle)**

The smiling baseball fan received the last ticket.

7. My sister's hair is scary looking. My sister's hair is pink. **(adjective)**

My sister's pink hair is scary looking.

8. Glinda ate a doughnut. It was filled with jelly. **(compound adjective)**

Glinda ate a jelly-filled doughnut.

Combining Sentences with a Series of Words or Phrases

The words *and, but, or, nor, for, so,* and *yet* (called *coordinating conjunctions*) are used to connect words, phrases, and clauses in writing. They are useful, but don't overuse them. You don't want your writing to ramble on and on.

The examples below combine shorter sentences using a series of words or phrases and a coordinating conjunction. (See page 513 in *Write Source* for more examples.)

Examples

Shorter Sentences:
My skateboard is new.
My skateboard is fast.
It's awesome.

Combined Sentence Using a Series of Words:
My skateboard is new, fast, and awesome.

Shorter Sentences:
Sam drinks milk at breakfast.
He drinks milk at lunch.
He drinks milk at dinner.

Combined Sentence Using a Series of Phrases:
Sam drinks milk at breakfast, at lunch, and at dinner.

Combine the following sets of short sentences into longer ones using the methods asked for in parentheses. The first one has been done for you.

1. The new policy seems unfair. The new policy seems impractical. The new policy seems confusing. **(Use a series of words.)**

   The new policy seems unfair, impractical, and confusing.

2. The kids built a clubhouse. They created club rules. They made up a secret handshake. **(Use a series of phrases.)**

The kids built a clubhouse, created club rules, and made up a secret handshake.

3. To earn money for her soccer club, Sarah sells magazines. She sells candy. She sells pizzas. **(Use a series of words.)**

To earn money for her soccer club, Sarah sells magazines, candy, and pizzas.

4. While dreaming, my dog Molly taps her front paws. While dreaming, she grins broadly. She also wags her tail. **(Use a series of phrases.)**

While dreaming, my dog Molly taps her front paws, grins broadly, and wags her tail.

5. Earning money is important to Landa. Participating in gymnastics is important to her. Painting people's portraits is also important to her. **(Use a series of phrases.)**

Earning money, participating in gymnastics, and painting people's portraits are important to Landa.

6. Andy loves sports and plays hockey. He plays baseball. He plays football. **(Use a series of words.)**

Andy loves sports and plays hockey, baseball, and football.

Next Step Pretend to be a mouse and describe some of the places a mouse can go (*in, out, over, under,* and so on). To do this, use eight prepositional phrases in one rambling sentence. Use "The mouse ran . . . " as the beginning of your sentence. (See the list of prepositions on page 742 in *Write Source*.) Don't forget to use commas to separate your prepositional phrases.

Combining Sentences with Compound Subjects and Predicates

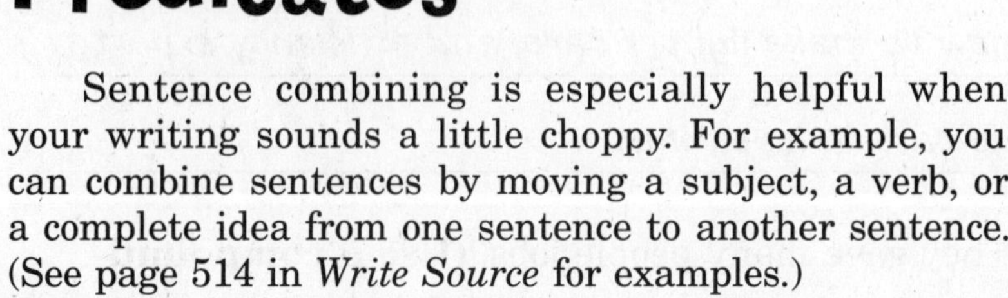

Sentence combining is especially helpful when your writing sounds a little choppy. For example, you can combine sentences by moving a subject, a verb, or a complete idea from one sentence to another sentence. (See page 514 in *Write Source* for examples.)

Directions **Combine the following sets of short sentences into longer ones using the methods asked for in parentheses. The first one has been done for you.**

1. Very few Americans owned a car 100 years ago. The Model T Ford changed all that. **(Use a compound sentence.)**

   Very few Americans owned a car 100 years ago, but the Model T Ford changed all that.

2. The Model T Ford was developed by Henry Ford. The Model T Ford was nicknamed "Tin Lizzie." **(Use a compound verb.)**

   The Model T Ford was developed by Henry Ford and nicknamed "Tin Lizzie."

3. A crude, boxlike body was used on this odd-looking car. Bicycle wheels were used on this odd-looking car. **(Use a compound subject.)**

   A crude, boxlike body and bicycle wheels were used on this odd-looking car.

4. The Tin Lizzie wasn't glamorous. The Tin Lizzie was cheap. **(Use a compound sentence.)**

   The Tin Lizzie wasn't glamorous, but it was cheap.

5. Ford produced about 10,000 Model T Fords between 1907 and 1908. He sold them for $850 each. **(Use a compound verb.)**

Ford produced about 10,000 Model T Fords between 1907 and 1908 and sold them for $850 each.

6. Engineers figured out how to make lighter cars. Efficiency experts figured out how to make cars in less time. **(Use a compound sentence.)**

Engineers figured out how to make lighter cars, and efficiency experts figured out how to make cars in less time.

7. Assembly lines cut costs. They gave many people jobs. **(Use a compound verb.)**

Assembly lines cut costs and gave many people jobs.

8. The Model T was a Ford design. The Model A was a Ford design, too. **(Use a compound subject.)**

The Model T and the Model A were Ford designs.

9. The car market forced the Ford Corporation to expand. The expansion increased profits. **(Use a compound sentence.)**

The car market forced the Ford Corporation to expand, and the expansion increased profits.

10. Ford planned to share company profits with his employees. He wanted to set a minimum wage. **(Use a compound verb.)**

Ford planned to share company profits with his employees and wanted to set a minimum wage.

Next Step Write freely for 5 minutes about a memorable car-related experience. Afterward, underline two sets of sentences that could be combined to make them more smooth reading. Combine these sentences on the back of your paper.

Kinds of Sentences 1

There are four kinds of sentences: *declarative, interrogative, imperative,* and *exclamatory.* A declarative sentence makes a statement. An interrogative sentence asks a question. An imperative sentence makes a request or gives a command. An exclamatory sentence communicates strong emotion. (To make sure you understand each kind of sentence, study the examples below and the ones on page 518 in *Write Source* for this information.)

Examples

Declarative:
Volcanoes have terrified people throughout history.

Interrogative:
Why are they so terrifying?

Imperative:
Read the following to find out.

Exclamatory:
You'll be amazed!

In the blank before each sentence, write "declarative," "interrogative," "imperative," or "exclamatory." The first sentence has been done for you.

interrogative **1.** Where are volcanoes most likely to occur?

imperative **2.** Read the following description to find out.

declarative **3.** Most volcanoes occur in a rim around the Pacific Ocean called the "ring of fire."

declarative **4.** Major eruptions are usually preceded by eruptions of steam and ash.

declarative **5.** The initial steam and ash eruptions are sort of like the volcano clearing its throat.

interrogative **6.** Do you know what happens next?

exclamatory **7.** Bang! The volcano blows its top!

declarative **8.** In other words, the magma erupts through the central and side vents.

interrogative **9.** What are some of the major volcanic eruptions throughout history?

declarative **10.** In 79 C.E., Mt. Vesuvius near Pompeii, Italy, erupted and killed about 2,000 fleeing people.

declarative **11.** Volcanoes erupted in Krakatoa (East Indies) in 1883, and more than 36,000 people died.

declarative **12.** In 1902, a volcanic explosion wiped out the entire community of St. Pierre on Martinique in the West Indies.

declarative **13.** The sole survivor was a man who was being held captive in a dungeon.

exclamatory **14.** That's incredible!

interrogative **15.** Is there anything that's good about volcanoes?

declarative **16.** Volcanic ash is very fertile, which is why many people have continued to live in the shadow of volcanoes over the years.

imperative **17.** Check the Internet or a good encyclopedia to find out more about volcanoes.

Next Step Find out more about one of the eruptions mentioned above (or another one). List at least three or four facts that you discover, and then use these facts in a paragraph about your subject. Try to use at least two kinds of sentences in your writing.

Kinds of Sentences 2

All sentences are either declarative, interrogative, imperative, or exclamatory. (To understand each kind, study the examples below and the ones on page 518 in *Write Source* for this information.)

Examples

Declarative:
Everyone has a weather story to share.

Interrogative:
What's your story?

Imperative:
Tell me about it.

Exclamatory:
No way, that didn't really happen!

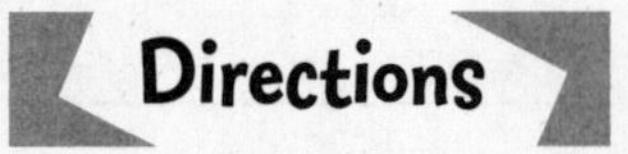

Write about weather in your part of the country using the four kinds of sentences. Be sure to use correct end punctuation.

Declarative ______________________________

____

Interrogative ______________________________

____

Imperative ______________________________

____

Exclamatory ______________________________

____

Directions You may never have experienced a tornado or dust storm. Then again, maybe you have! In any case, everyone has had a specific experience with the weather that would make a good story. Think about a time when you were in the middle of a bad storm, watched snow pile up in a blizzard, saw the aftermath of a hurricane or a flood, and so on. Describe that experience in a paragraph of 5 to 8 sentences. Use at least three kinds of sentences in your description.

Next Step Add an illustration to your paragraph and, as a class, post your work around the classroom.

Types of Sentences

There are three basic types of sentences: simple sentences, compound sentences, and complex sentences. (See the examples below plus the ones on pages 515–517 in *Write Source* for this information.)

Examples

Simple Sentences:

I dug a huge hole.

(one subject; one verb)

Dad found and bought the perfect tree.

(one subject; compound verb)

Dad and I placed the tree in the hole.

(compound subject; one verb)

Compound Sentence:

I quickly filled in the hole, and Dad gave the tree a good watering.

(two independent clauses joined by a comma plus "and")

Complex Sentence:

After we finished our work, we admired the new tree.

(one dependent clause, "after we finished our work," plus one independent clause, "we admired the new tree")

Identify each sentence below by writing either "simple," "compound," or "complex" on the blank space. The first sentence has been done for you.

compound **1.** Forests once covered two-thirds of the earth, but now they cover only one-third of the earth.

simple **2.** We need forests to survive.

simple **3.** We breathe in oxygen and give off carbon dioxide.

complex **4.** Trees are just the opposite because they absorb carbon dioxide and give off oxygen.

compound 5. This is a great arrangement for humans, and we should all be grateful to the trees.

simple 6. Trees are cut down for houses, paper, fuel, lumber, and other uses.

complex 7. If enough trees are cut down, animal species begin to disappear.

compound 8. Trees hold the soil in place, and soil erosion is then reduced.

complex 9. When the wind blows, trees can serve as effective windbreaks.

compound 10. Forests offer valuable shelter for wildlife, and they provide innumerable recreation areas for people.

complex 11. Although there are about 20,000 kinds of trees, only 1,000 kinds grow in the United States.

simple 12. Each year the average American uses wood products equal to a 100-foot-tall tree.

simple 13. People throughout the world eat fruit, nuts, and other tree products.

complex 14. The bark of the cinchona tree contains quinine, which doctors use to treat malaria.

complex 15. All of us should plant a tree every year so that we can maintain a good supply of beautiful trees.

Next Step *What would your life be like without trees?* Write a paragraph in which you answer this question in detail. Afterward, identify your first four sentences as either "simple," "compound," or "complex." Share your results.

Compound Sentences 1

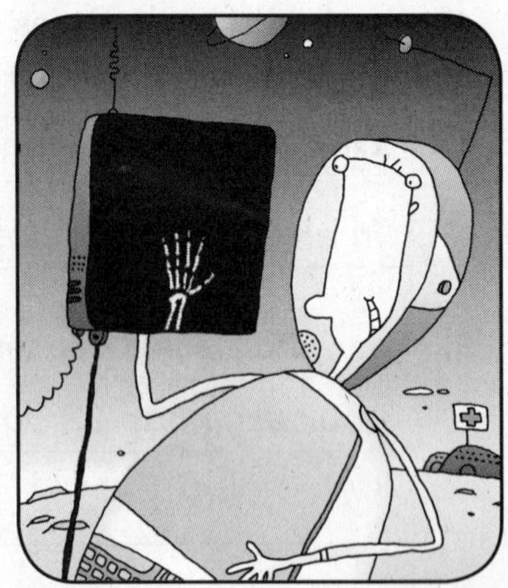

A compound sentence is made up of two or more simple sentences joined by a comma and a coordinating conjunction, by punctuation, or by both. (See page 516 and 744.2 in *Write Source* for more information and a list of coordinating conjunctions.) The examples below show you how compound sentences can be formed.

Examples

The skeleton gives your body shape, but it also protects your vital organs.
(In this compound sentence, a comma and the coordinating conjunction "but" connect the two simple sentences.)

Your body framework is vital to life; learn as much as you can about it.
(In this compound sentence, a semicolon connects the two simple sentences.)

Turn each set of simple sentences into a compound sentence using a comma and a coordinating conjunction. For the first three sets of sentences, use the coordinating conjunction in parentheses. The first one has been done for you.

1. Your skeleton is invisible. It never lets you down. **(yet)**

   Your skeleton is invisible, yet it never lets you down.

2. Without your skeleton, you would be unable to move. Your muscles would have nothing to attach themselves to. **(for)**

   Without your skeleton, you would be unable to move, for your muscles would have nothing to attach themselves to.

3. An adult person has 206 bones. A baby may have as many as 270. **(but)**

   An adult person has 206 bones, but a baby may have as many as 270.

4. Gradually, some bones in a child's body fuse together. This results in an adult with fewer bones.

   Gradually, some bones in a child's body fuse together, and this results in an adult with fewer bones.

5. Your skull has 22 bones. Only the lower jaw is movable.

   Your skull has 22 bones, yet only the lower jaw is movable.

6. Your skull bones protect your brain and eyes. The bones in your rib cage protect your heart and lungs.

   Your skull bones protect your brain and eyes, and the bones in your rib cage protect your heart and lungs.

7. The longest bone in the body is the thighbone. It is also the strongest.

   The longest bone in the body is the thighbone, and it is also the strongest.

8. The tiniest bones in the body are the three bones in your middle ear. Without them, you couldn't hear.

   The tiniest bones in the body are the three bones in your middle ear, but without them, you couldn't hear.

Next Step List the following names of bones on your paper: *clavicle, sternum, phallanges, patella, tibia,* and *tarsals*. Then write the location of each type of bone next to its name. You may need to study a diagram of a human skeleton. Use this information to write three pairs of simple sentences. Exchange papers with a classmate and try combining the sentence pairs into compound sentences.

Compound Sentences 2

You can use a comma and a coordinating conjunction to connect simple sentences. The conjunction you choose shows the relationship of the ideas in the two parts of the new sentence. Be sure to choose the conjunction that has the meaning you want. The conjunctions are *and, but, or, nor, for, so,* and *yet*. Be sure to choose the right conjunction for each sentence. (See page 516 and 744.1 in *Write Source* for more information.)

Example

Many people live in the northern part of the United States, but some complain that there is too little daylight during the winter.
(The conjunction with the best meaning is "but.")

Write the correct conjunction for each of the following compound sentences. The first one has been done for you.

1. Some people say 45 degrees is cold, ___but___ *(or, so, but, and)* others say 0 degrees is cold.

2. Snow can make roads slippery, ___so___ *(or, so, yet)* drivers need to slow down in a snowstorm.

3. Winter in northern states can be six months long, ___and___ *(or, but, and)* it can be very windy and cold.

4. It is possible to walk on thick ice, ___yet___ *(so, yet, and)* even thick ice can have weak spots.

5. If you walk outside in strong winds and cold temperatures, you should wear a good hat, ___or___ *(or, so, but, and)* you might get frostbitten ears.

Directions Check the underlined conjunctions in the following compound sentences. If a sentence does not make sense with the conjunction, add one from the list below. If it does make sense, write the word "correct" above it. The first one has been done for you.

and but for nor or so yet

correct
1. James wanted to swim on Wednesday, <u>but</u> the water was too cold.

nor
2. I really don't like scary movies, <u>or</u> do I care for violent TV shows.

but
3. Jesse delivers papers on weekends, <u>and</u> he can't deliver them on school days.

or
4. One choice is to buy the bike, <u>and</u> you can save your money for the class trip.

correct
5. The bus was late, <u>so</u> the students sat on the grass near the bus stop.

correct
6. Workers had measured carefully, <u>yet</u> one leg of the bench was too long.

or
7. With only one night free this week, Sally could see the new movie, <u>and</u> she could go to the dance.

so
8. Mercury is the closest planet to the sun, <u>but</u> it has the shortest year.

Next Step Write several compound sentences about the weather. Use the conjunctions "and," "so," "but," and "or."

Complex Sentences 1

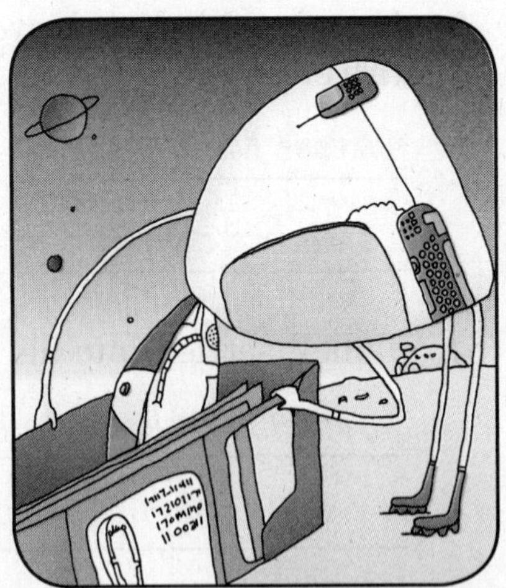

You can combine two simple sentences into a complex sentence using subordinating conjunctions such as *after, although, before,* and *unless*. Note how a subordinating conjunction is used to combine two simple ideas in the following examples. (See page 517 and 746.1 in *Write Source* for more examples.)

Examples

Simple Sentences:
Jon checked his wallet for money. He bought the best-selling thriller.

Combined into a Complex Sentence:
Jon checked his wallet for money before he bought the best-selling thriller.
(The subordinating conjunction "before" connects the two ideas.)

Simple Sentences:
Katrice studied her math. Amika read a short story in her literature book.

Combined into a Complex Sentence:
While Katrice studied her math, Amika read a short story in her literature book.
(The subordinating conjunction "while" connects the two ideas.)

Note: If the group of words introduced by a subordinating conjunction comes at the beginning of a sentence, a comma is placed after the introductory clause.

Directions **Combine the following sets of short sentences into complex sentences. Use the subordinating conjunctions given in parentheses for the first four sentences. The first one has been done for you.**

1. The rope-and-wood bridge collapsed. Joe stood and watched. **(as)**

   The rope-and-wood bridge collapsed as Joe stood and watched.

2. The first colonists looked to England for help. It had been their home. **(because)**

   The first colonists looked to England for help because it had been their home.

3. Maurice filled his bicycle tires with air. He pedaled to the south side of town. **(after)**

After Maurice filled his bicycle tires with air, he pedaled to the south side of town.

4. Jamell settled into his favorite fishing spot. The sun came up. **(as)**

Jamell settled into his favorite fishing spot as the sun came up.

5. Scotty stopped running. He heard the police officer shout.

Scotty stopped running when he heard the police officer shout.

6. Two feet of snow fell. Reva made it home.

Although two feet of snow fell, Reva made it home.

7. You're all set to go to camp. You haven't registered properly.

You're all set to go to camp unless you haven't registered properly.

8. Rosario checked on the two children. She fell asleep.

After Rosario checked on the two children, she fell asleep.

Next Step Write freely for 5 minutes about what happened yesterday afternoon between the time you were dismissed from your last class and the time you sat down to dinner. Put in as much detail as you can. Then exchange your writing with a classmate. Note two sets of sentences in each other's work that could be combined. When your paper is returned, try connecting the marked sets of sentences as you did above.

Complex Sentences 2

You can combine two simple sentences into a complex sentence using adjective clauses. An adjective clause is one that begins with a word like *who, which,* or *that* (called *relative pronouns*). Combining ideas with these words will help you cut down on unnecessary repetition in your writing. (To learn how this is done, study the examples below as well as the examples on page 517 and 746.1 in *Write Source*.)

Examples

Simple Sentences:
The radio station played unfamiliar songs.
The radio station was geared for an older audience.

Combined into a Complex Sentence:
The radio station, which was geared for an older audience, played unfamiliar songs.
(By combining the two ideas with "which," the unnecessary repetition of "radio station" is avoided.)

Simple Sentences:
The newspaper gives detailed statistics for major league baseball.
The newspaper is delivered to our school.

Combined into a Complex Sentence:
The newspaper that is delivered to our school gives detailed statistics for major league baseball.
(By combining the two ideas with "that," the unnecessary repetition of "newspaper" is avoided.)

Combine the following pairs of simple sentences into one complex sentence. In each case, a relative pronoun, other key words, and punctuation marks have already been put into place. The first one has been done for you.

1. The tall mail carrier delivers on Wednesdays. The tall mail carrier is my uncle.

The tall mail carrier who *delivers on Wednesdays* is *my uncle* .

2. The waitress works at the corner cafe. She looks sad and weary.

The waitress who *works at the corner cafe* looks *sad and weary*.

3. The pink Cadillac was parked in the driveway. The pink Cadillac convertible was dented by hail.

The pink Cadillac convertible that *was parked in the driveway* was dented *by hail*.

4. The statue stood by the birdbath in the garden. It was stolen.

The statue that *stood by the birdbath in the garden* was *stolen*.

5. Pluto is the most distant planet in our solar system. It takes 248 years to orbit the sun.

Pluto, which *takes 248 years to orbit the sun*, is *the most distant planet in our solar system*.

6. The extreme heat affected the runners. The runners were participating in the conference relays.

The extreme heat *affected the runners* who were *participating in the conference relays*.

7. John's half-eaten apple is a Golden Delicious. The apple is now totally brown.

John's half-eaten apple, which is now *totally brown*, is *a Golden Delicious*.

Next Step Turn to *Write Source* and find out when you should use "who/which/that." Discuss the results of your research with a classmate.

Expanding Sentences

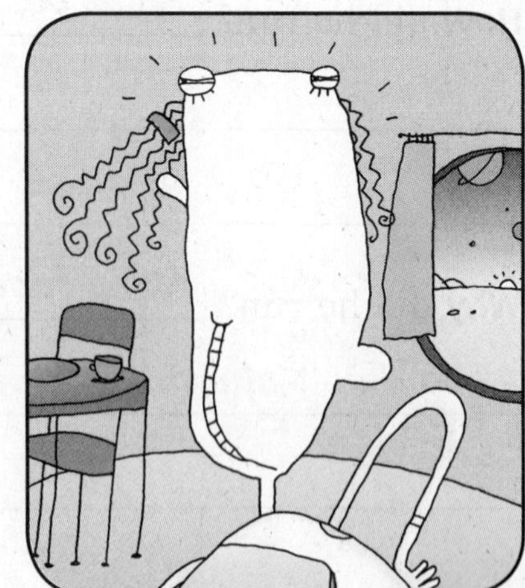

You needn't pack specific facts and details into all of your sentences in a piece of writing. That would be overdoing it. But, it's also true that you will not hold a reader's attention if most of your sentences lack detail. Note the two sentences that follow. (See page 519 in *Write Source* for more information.)

Examples

John ate the pancakes.

As his sister watched, **John ate the stack of pancakes** in a single bite.

The basic idea is the same in both sentences: *John ate the pancakes.* However, the second sentence is expanded with more specific detail. It shows when and how John ate the pancakes.

Carefully note below the process of expanding a sentence.

The basic sentence:	**Karlene smiled.**
When did she smile?	This morning, **Karlene smiled.**
How did she smile?	**This morning, Karlene smiled** slyly.
Why did she smile?	**This morning, Karlene smiled slyly** as her brother sat in the scrambled eggs.

Now you try it. Build the following basic idea into an expanded sentence.

(Answers will vary.)

The basic sentence: **Sidney ran.**

When did he run? *All at once, Sidney ran.*

____

____

Where did he run (in what location), or what was his destination?

All at once, Sidney ran away from the dog.

____

How did he run? *All at once, Sidney ran helter-skelter away from the dog.*

Why did he run? *All at once, Sidney ran helter-skelter away from the dog who didn't approve of trespassers on his owner's property.*

Sentence Expanding Revisited

Carefully read and evaluate your newly expanded sentence. Decide if it contains too little, too much, or just enough detail. Rewrite it below, trying to make it even better. (Your sentence doesn't have to answer all of the questions asked above.) Share your results with a classmate.

Revised Expanded Sentence:

Next Step Write three basic ideas that could be starting points for additional expanded sentences. Exchange these ideas with a classmate for more sentence-expanding practice.

Expanding Sentences with Phrases

Ideas from short sentences can be combined into longer units of thought by moving a phrase from one sentence to the other. (To learn how to combine sentences in this way, see pages 519–520 in *Write Source*.)

Examples

Shorter Sentences:
The spaghetti sauce tastes burned. It is on the stove.

Combined Sentence Using a Prepositional Phrase:
The spaghetti sauce on the stove tastes burned.

Shorter Sentences:
Bruce was actually reading a book. Bruce is a self-proclaimed book hater.

Combined Sentence Using an Appositive Phrase:
Bruce, a self-proclaimed book hater, was actually reading a book.

Combine each pair of simple sentences using the phrase asked for in parentheses. The first one has been done for you.

1. It was April 5, 2004. I got my braces off. **(prepositional phrase)**

   On April 5, 2004, I got my braces off.

2. My first-grade teacher loved to play Simon Says. My first-grade teacher's name was Mr. Simon. **(appositive phrase)**

   Mr. Simon, my first-grade teacher,

   loved to play Simon Says.

3. Johanna won two medals last week. She's a first-rate gymnast. **(appositive phrase)**

   Johanna, a first-rate gymnast, won two medals last week.

4. Manuel is studying. He's at the library. **(prepositional phrase)**

   Manuel is studying at the library.

5. Mike cheerfully volunteered to help his little brother. His little brother needed help with his math homework. **(prepositional phrase)**

   Mike cheerfully volunteered to help his little brother with his math homework.

6. Todd goes to the movies twice a week. He's the neighborhood movie freak. **(appositive phrase)**

   Todd, the neighborhood movie freak, goes to the movies twice a week.

Next Step In the space below, write one original sentence naming six members of your family (aunts, uncles, cousins, grandparents, or pets may be included) or six people who live in your neighborhood. Use an appositive phrase for each name (Cheeks, my fuzzy hamster; Libby, my older sister; . . . are all in my family).

Expanding Sentences with Phrases and Clauses

Using a variety of sentence lengths, and combining shorter thoughts into smooth, longer sentences, can make your writing easier and more interesting to read. (Turn to the sentence-combining section on pages 519–520 in *Write Source* for explanations and examples.)

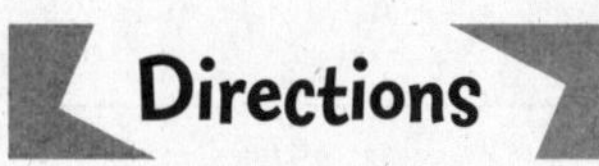

Combine each pair of simple sentences using the type of phrase asked for in parentheses. The first one has been done for you.

1. For centuries, people have traveled between England and France. They traveled by boat. **(prepositional phrase)**

   For centuries, people have traveled between England and France by boat.

2. Nowadays, they can ride a train through the "Chunnel." The Chunnel is a tunnel under the water between England and France. **(appositive phrase)**

   Nowadays, they can ride a train through the "Chunnel," a tunnel under the water between England and France.

3. People can take their cars. They take their cars aboard the train. **(prepositional phrase)**

   People can take their cars aboard the train.

4. The Chunnel trip is 31 miles long. It is a half-hour ride across the channel. **(appositive phrase)**

   The Chunnel trip, a half-hour ride across the channel, is 31 miles long.

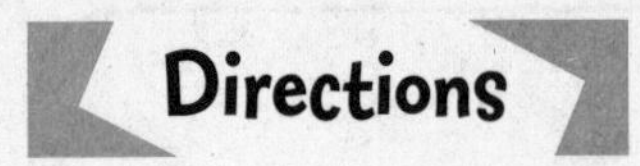

Combine the following sets of simple sentences into complex sentences using the relative pronouns given in parentheses. *Note:* Use commas in your combined sentences where necessary.

1. The Chunnel runs under the English Channel. The English Channel separates England from the European continent. **(which)**

   The Chunnel runs under the English Channel, which separates England from the European continent.

2. The Chunnel trains are among the fastest in Europe. They travel at speeds of up to 186 miles per hour. **(which)**

   The Chunnel trains, which travel at speeds of up to 186 miles per hour, are among the fastest in Europe.

3. Europeans have discussed a land crossing to England since the time of Napoleon. Napoleon was emperor of France in the early 1800s. **(who)**

   Europeans have discussed a land crossing to England since the time of Napoleon, who was emperor of France in the early 1800s.

4. London's Chunnel station is named after the town of Waterloo. Napoleon was defeated at Waterloo in June 1815. **(where)**

   London's Chunnel station is named after the town of Waterloo, where Napoleon was defeated in June 1815.

5. Napolcon was defeated by the Duke of Wellington. Wellington was a British soldier and statesman. **(who)**

   Napoleon was defeated by the Duke of Wellington, who was a British soldier and statesman.

Next Step In your class, see who can write the longest complex sentence. Be sure to use relative pronouns and punctuation correctly.

Sentence Variety Review 1

Combine the following sets of short sentences into single, longer ones. Combine each set using the method asked for in parentheses. (See pages 511–520 in *Write Source* for help.) The first one has been done for you.

1. Daisy drank a quart of milk. Then she sat down to dinner.
(Use a subordinating conjunction.)
After Daisy drank a quart of milk, she sat down to dinner.

2. Katie goes swimming every day. Josh goes swimming every day.
(Use a compound subject.)
Katie and Josh go swimming every day.

3. The snake is long. He is strong. The snake is dangerous.
(Use a series of words.)
The snake is long, strong, and dangerous.

4. My mom always pulled the weeds. They still took over her garden.
(Use a subordinating conjunction.)
Although my mom always pulled the weeds, they still took over her garden.

5. The hostess took us to our table. She handed us menus.
(Use a compound verb.)
The hostess took us to our table and handed us menus.

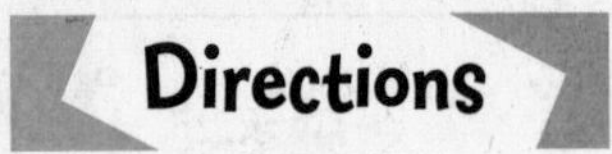

Combine the following sets of simple sentences and then finish the story on your own paper. Key words and punctuation marks are included in each sentence to help you with your work. The first combined sentence has been done for you.

1. Rachel's heart was pounding. She stood watching the softball game.

Rachel's heart was pounding as she stood watching the softball game.

2. This was the third game of the season. Rachel still hadn't gotten to play.

This was the third game of the season, and

Rachel still hadn't gotten to play.

3. She should have been sitting on the bench. She was too anxious to sit still.

She should have been sitting on the bench, but

she was too anxious to sit still.

4. Rachel was small for her age. She had been practicing hard and was eager to help her team win.

Although *Rachel was small for her age*,

she had *been practicing hard and was eager to help her team win*

.

5. The fifth inning started. Coach Suarez looked down the bench. He saw Rachel.

When *the fifth inning started*,

Coach Suarez *looked down the bench* and

saw Rachel. The coach also saw Sonja

next to her. He had to decide . . . **(Finish on your own paper.)**

Next Step Exchange stories with a classmate. Check each other's work for shorter sentences that could be combined like those you created above.

Sentence Variety Review 2

Combine the following sets of shorter sentences into single, longer ones. Combine each set using the method asked for in parentheses. (See pages 511–520 in *Write Source* for help.) The first one has been done for you.

1. Breaking an arm or a leg hurts. Spraining a wrist or an ankle is also painful. **(Use a compound sentence.)**

   Breaking an arm or a leg hurts, but spraining a wrist or an ankle is also painful.

2. These injuries aren't life threatening, but they are often very painful. These injuries are common. **(Use a key word.)**

   These common injuries aren't life threatening, but they are often very painful.

3. "It's just a sprain," they say. Your ankle swells and turns an ugly purple color. **(Use a subordinating conjunction.)**

   "It's just a sprain," they say as your ankle swells and turns an ugly purple color.

4. What is a sprain? What causes it to happen? **(Use a compound sentence.)**

   What is a sprain, and what causes it to happen?

5. Ligaments hold your bones together at the joints. Ligaments are bands of strong tissue. **(Use an appositive phrase.)**

   Ligaments, bands of strong tissue, hold your bones together at the joints.

6. Your shoulders have joints. Your elbows have joints. Your knees have joints. **(Use a series of words.)**

Your shoulders, elbows, and knees have joints.

7. You're running at top speed. Suddenly you stop, pivot, jump, and then land with a "Yeow!" **(Use a subordinating conjunction.)**

You're running at top speed when suddenly you stop, pivot, jump, and then land with a "Yeow!"

8. Your knee joint moves too far. The ligaments stretch or tear. **(Use a relative pronoun.)**

Your knee joint moves too far, which stretches or tears the ligaments.

9. Ice decreases the pain. It decreases swelling. It decreases injury to the tissue. **(Use a series of words.)**

Ice decreases the pain, swelling, and injury to the tissue.

10. Reach for an ice pack. Reach for a can of frozen fruit juice or for a bag of frozen peas if nothing else is available. **(Use a series of phrases.)**

Reach for an ice pack, a can of frozen fruit juice, or a bag of frozen peas if nothing else is available.

Next Step Make a list of phrases that describe an injury you have had. Then combine the phrases into sentences to summarize your experience.

Parts of Speech
Activities

Every activity includes a main practice section in which you learn about or review the different parts of speech. Most of the activities include helpful *Write Source* references. In addition, the **Next Step** activities give you follow-up practice with certain skills.

Nouns	**123**
Pronouns	**133**
Verbs	**141**
Adjectives	**159**
Adverbs	**167**
Prepositions	**171**
Interjections	**173**
Conjunctions	**175**
Parts of Speech	**180**

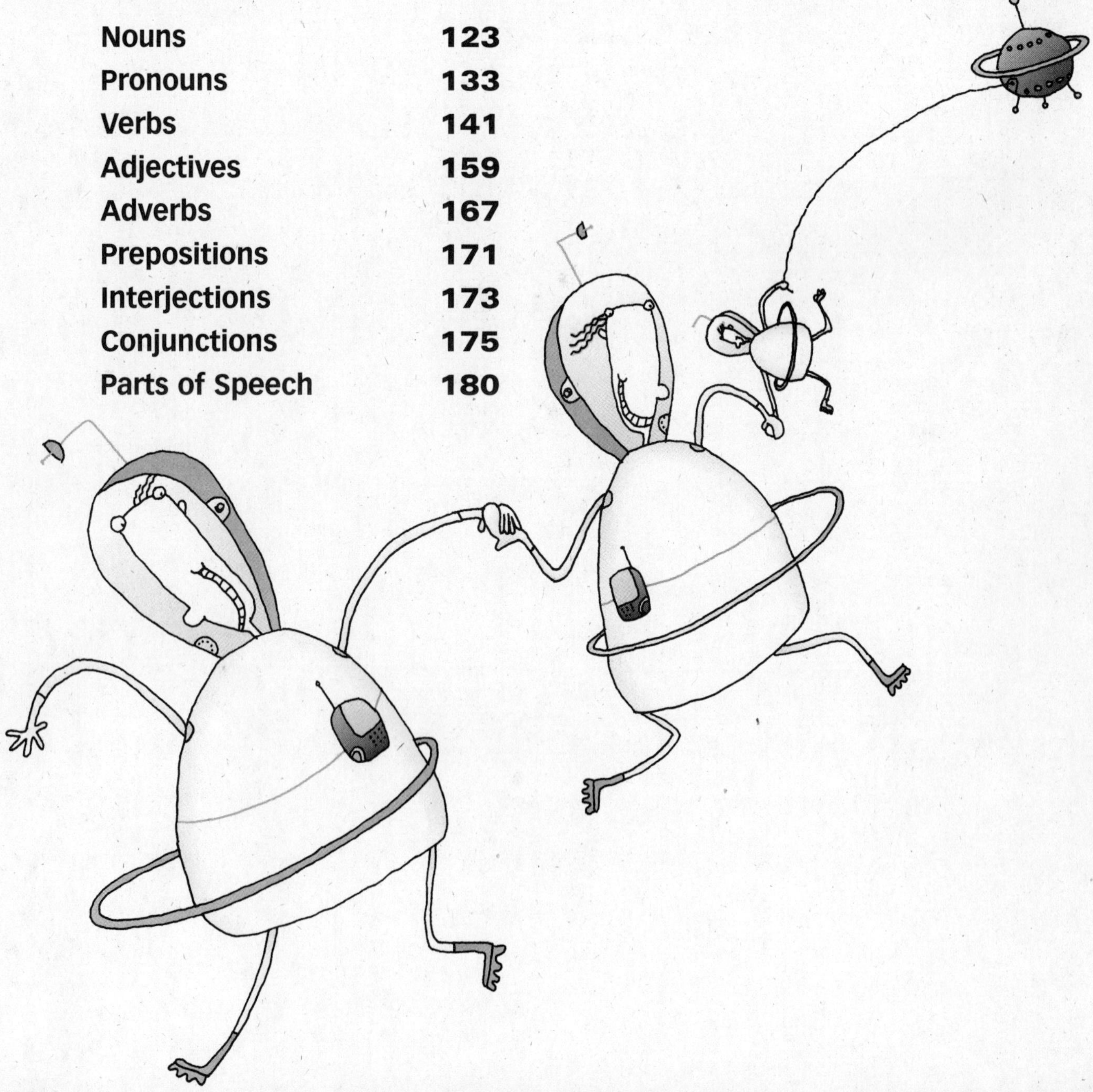

Nouns

Nouns name the people, places, things, or ideas we use in our writing and speaking. Note the nouns (color) in the example sentence. (See pages 470 and 702 in *Write Source* for more examples.)

Example

Sally met her new classmates in the hallway.

"Sally" names a person, "classmates" names the people who have gathered around her, and "hallway" names the place where they stand. "Sally" is also the subject of the example sentence. (The subject is the part of a sentence that is doing something or about which something is said.)

Underline the nouns used as simple subjects in the sentences that follow. In the space provided, tell whether each subject (noun) is a "person," a "place," a "thing," or an "idea." The first one has been done for you.

idea **1.** The thought of introducing herself made Sally feel queasy.

person **2.** The students stared at her.

idea **3.** Her nervousness was obvious to everyone.

thing **4.** The first-hour bell scared Sally.

person **5.** The teachers told all the students to get to their first-hour classes.

person **6.** Sally had no idea which way to go.

place **7.** McKinley School was so much larger than her old school.

person **8.** Two girls walked up to Sally, smiled, and offered to help.

person **9.** Sally breathed a sigh of relief and thanked the girls.

place **10.** Her first-hour classroom was down the hall.

Next Step Write one sentence that includes four nouns, one used as a person, one as a place, one as a thing, and one as an idea.

Singular and Plural Nouns

A **singular noun** names one person, place, thing, or idea. A **plural noun** names more than one person, place, thing, or idea at 704.1–704.2 in *Write Source*.)

Examples

Big celebrations are held every Fourth of July.
("Celebrations" is a plural noun. "Fourth of July" is a singular noun.)

Many families have a picnic on this day.
("Families" is a plural noun. "Picnic" and "day" are singular nouns.)

Underline all of the nouns in the sentences that follow. Write "S" above each singular noun and "P" above each plural noun. (The number of nouns in each sentence is given in parentheses.)

1. One celebration was held in the field behind the Bunde Methodist Church. *(3)*
2. That church is in the country, about three miles from town. *(4)*
3. There were games and contests with prizes all day. *(4)*
4. The women from the Ladies Aid Society were competing by having each lady pound a handful of huge spikes into a thick beam. *(6)*
5. A relay with suitcases for the men always made the people laugh. *(4)*
6. Another relay for the men entertained everybody. *(2)*
7. The women watched the men racing to hang laundry on the clotheslines. *(4)*
8. Shirts hanging by their sleeves looked strange. *(2)*

Next Step Write five sentences about a Fourth of July you remember. Exchange your sentences with a classmate. Underline and identify each singular and plural noun.

Common and Proper Nouns

A **proper noun** is the name of a specific person, place, thing, or idea. Proper nouns are capitalized. A **common noun** is any noun that does not name a specific person, place, thing, or idea. Common nouns are not capitalized. (See the examples below plus the ones at 702.1–702.2 in *Write Source*.)

Example

Jim bought a new car from a rental company.

"Jim" is a proper noun that names a specific person.
The words "car" and "company" are common nouns that name things.

Directions **Underline each noun in the sentences below. Write "C" above each common noun. Write "P" above each proper noun. (The number of nouns in each sentence is given in parentheses.)**

1. A company that rents cars must care for them. *(2)*
2. Each engine receives good care and regular service. *(3)*
3. Most rental cars stand outdoors, winter and summer. *(4)*
4. This car, a black station wagon, just received a coat of wax. *(4)*
5. Jim waxed it yesterday morning, on the last Thursday in July. *(4)*
6. He has no idea when his car will receive its next coat of wax. *(4)*
7. Jim drove the car for the first time last week. *(4)*
8. The car performed well in traffic, especially on the highway. *(3)*
9. He took his friend Paul Block and his son to Chicago to watch the Cubs play baseball. *(6)*
10. They parked the car in Skokie and rode the train to Wrigley Field. *(4)*

Directions In each sentence below, fill in the first blank with a common noun and fill in the second blank with a proper noun. The first sentence has been done for you. *(Answers will vary.)*

1. If I could buy a *sound system*, I would buy one made by *Sony*.
2. Alisha plays *volleyball* on a team called the *Troy Tigers*.
3. Josh got a new *golden retriever*; he named it *Sherlock*.
4. Terri is reading a *book* about the history of *Egypt*.
5. We watched a *movie* called *Llama Trauma*.
6. I had to go to the *dentist* last *Friday*.
7. Sasha was born in the *middle* of *August*.
8. My favorite *name* is *Helaine*.
9. Michael likes *gum*, but only if it's *Double Bubble Blocks*.
10. Shavon visited *an amusement park*, which is located in *Missouri*.

Next Step Write a poem in which all of the nouns are proper nouns. You can use any of the types of poems in *Write Source* or a form of your own.

Concrete and Abstract Nouns

Nouns can be concrete or abstract. A **concrete noun** names a thing that is physical (can be touched or seen). An **abstract noun** names something you can think about but cannot see or touch. (Study the examples that follow as well as the ones at 702.3–702.4 in *Write Source*.)

Examples

Concrete Nouns:

Andes Mountains **Venus** **pickles** **dirt**

Abstract Nouns:

Buddhism **hope** **prejudice**

Read the following passage and underline all the nouns. Above each noun write "C" for concrete or "A" for abstract. The first sentence has been done for you.

Have you ever visited the mountains? Theories about how mountains formed are interesting, but I'd rather visit the mountains than study them. My belief is that the mountains are there for enjoyment, and I think that's a good enough reason for their existence. My dream is to visit the Andes Mountains in South America. The most amazing fact about the Andes is that they are the longest chain of mountains in the world. They are a natural wonder that stretches more than 4,500 miles. They spread throughout seven countries from Venezuela to Chile. I would like to climb the Andes, but there is less oxygen in the mountains, and I may end up out of breath.

Read the following paragraph. Underline all the nouns. Then list each concrete and abstract noun in the correct column below. (Compare lists with a classmate.)

I have to give a speech today. I will talk about fear because I am afraid to speak in front of the class. Someone said that bravery is doing something even though you are afraid. I hope I will have that feeling of bravery when I am done. Our teacher told us we have to speak for three minutes. I think that scares me the most. What can I say so my classmates will listen to me? Maybe I can get them to share their own thoughts. If I interview some of them, I will know what scares them. I read that people often fear things they shouldn't worry about like getting hit by lightning. I wonder if my friends are like that?

Concrete	Abstract
class	speech
teacher	fear
classmates	front
people	bravery
lightning	something
friends	feeling
	bravery
	minutes
	thoughts
	things

Next Step Where do you find peace? Write a paragraph that describes a place where you feel secure and peaceful. Circle any abstract nouns in your writing.

Using Nouns

Nouns are often identified by their use in a sentence. A subject noun is the subject of a sentence. A predicate noun follows a form of the *be* verb and renames the subject. A possessive noun shows ownership or possession. An object noun is used as a direct object, an indirect object, or the object of a preposition. (To learn more about the uses of nouns, study the examples below as well as the examples at 704.4–704.7 in *Write Source*.)

Examples

Subject Noun:
Hollywood produces many films.

Predicate Noun:
My town is the capital.

Possessive Noun:
My town's major asset is its people.

Object Noun:
You'll enjoy my town.

Identify the use of the underlined noun in each sentence. Choose one of the following labels: "S" for subject, "P" for predicate noun, "PN" for possessive noun, and "O" for object noun. The first one has been done for you.

1. I have some exciting news.
2. Hollywood has discovered Burlington, my hometown!
3. The film crew arrived to shoot a movie.
4. Ms. Peres and Mr. Snyder, local people from my community, have been hired as assistants.
5. The mayor's face lit up when the announcement was made on local TV.
6. Our newspaper is providing full local coverage.

7. Two rising film stars have the lead roles.

8. Two of the "extras" that were hired are Miguel Gomez and Amika Jons.

9. These two people are citizens in our community right now.

10. My life is much more exciting since Hollywood came to town.

11. If I were a Hollywood producer, I'd do a film about animals.

12. This experience is great for Burlington's identity.

13. Four blocks in the center of town will be the primary area for the filming.

14. Dimitri Karas's house is right in the middle of this area.

15. I've never felt so much excitement in our town.

Next Step Write four sentences about your city or town. Each sentence should highlight an interesting, a fun, or an unusual point of interest. Try to label one example for each use of a noun.

Specific Nouns

Specific nouns help writers create clear images or word pictures for their readers. Can you recognize award-winning, specific nouns when you see them? To find out, read the two columns of nouns that follow. (See page 471 in *Write Source* for more information about specific nouns.)

Examples

General Nouns	Specific Nouns
shelter	**pup tent**
poultry	**duck**
animal	**wombat**
campground	**Camp Runamuck**
lake	**Mud Lake**

Directions **In the sentences below, replace the underlined general nouns with specific nouns. Use nouns that will make the sentences very interesting. The first sentence has been done for you.** *(Answers will vary.)*

1. I want a lot of onions on my ~~sandwich~~ *hamburger* and a lot of sugar in my ~~drink~~ *iced tea*.

2. Our classroom has some fish in a container.

3. Jerry found an animal hiding under his bed at camp.

4. A person rang our doorbell at night.

5. Rosa and I made dessert and then played a game.

6. My uncle raises vegetables and flowers.

7. Sam dived into the water wearing his clothes.

8. A person leaped out of the car and ran into the building.

Next Step Trade papers with a classmate and read each other's sentences. Note the specific nouns your classmate used and how those nouns made his or her sentences different from yours.

Directions **List at least 10 interesting or important nouns. Look in a dictionary, a thesaurus, or *Write Source* for award-winning nouns. Also notice appealing nouns as you read books, magazines, and advertisements. How will you know whether or not a noun is "award-winning"? Some suggestions follow:**

It might be the *sound* of certain words that attracts you.
(I like the way the words mozzarella cheese roll off my tongue.)

Maybe the *feeling* a noun gives you is important.
(The word willow gives me a good feeling.)

Then again, maybe a noun has a special meaning for you.
(The word geranium has a special meaning for me because every summer my grandmother has these flowers on her porch.)

1. ______________________________

2. ______________________________

3. ______________________________

4. ______________________________

5. ______________________________

6. ______________________________

7. ______________________________

8. ______________________________

9. ______________________________

10. ______________________________

Next Step Share your work with a classmate. Discuss which words you like in each other's list. Use one of your favorite nouns as the starting point for a clustering activity. (See "Clustering" on page 544 in *Write Source* for guidelines and a model.)

Pronouns

Pronouns are words used in place of nouns. They allow us to communicate clearly and smoothly. Most of the pronouns we use are personal pronouns (*I, we, they, he, her,* and so on), but there are other types as well. The following sentence reveals the importance of pronouns in our language. (See pages 706–714 in *Write Source* to find out about all types of pronouns.)

Example

Sentence without Pronouns:

Mr. Lee thought that Mr. Lee should write Mr. Lee's name on the board.
(Repeating the noun "Mr. Lee" sounds a little strange.)

Sentence with Pronouns:

Mr. Lee thought that he should write his name on the board.
(Using the pronouns "he" and "his" for "Mr. Lee" makes this sentence smoother and easier to understand.)

Underline the personal pronouns in the following sentences. (The number of personal pronouns in each sentence is given in parentheses.) The first one has been done for you.

1. My parents asked our elderly neighbor to plant some trees for us. *(3)*
2. He dug two ash saplings out of his yard; they had grown there wild. *(3)*
3. In early spring, he came with them, their roots neatly balled in burlap. *(3)*
4. I watched as he skillfully planted those trees, his hands knowing exactly what to do. *(3)*
5. Their branches were full of leaf buds. *(1)*
6. "When you transplant a tree," he said, "you must leave the taproot as long as possible." *(3)*
7. With his feet, he firmly pressed down the soil around the roots. *(2)*
8. As he put his tools away, we asked him in for a cup of coffee. *(4)*

Antecedents

The word that a pronoun replaces is called the *antecedent*. If the antecedent is singular, the pronoun must be singular; if it is plural, the pronoun must be plural. (Study the examples below as well as the ones on page 478 and 706.1 in *Write Source*.)

Examples

The players won (*his/their*) matches.
(The antecedent "players" is plural, so the pronoun must be plural.)

A soldier may one day become an officer if (*he or she/they*) is dedicated.
(The antecedent "soldier" is singular, so the pronoun must be singular.)

Underline the correct pronoun in parentheses. Then draw an arrow to its antecedent. (Use "*him or her*," "*his or hers*," and so on, when either a male or female could be referred to by the antecedent.)

1. Both magazines offered *(its / their)* customers a good deal.

2. The boss will hire anyone if *(he or she / they)* can work on weekends.

3. Paula and Rosa brought samples of *(her / their)* winning recipe.

4. The club decided to raise *(its / their)* membership dues.

5. Not everyone should do weight lifting in *(his or her / their)* exercise program. (*Everyone* is a singular antecedent.)

6. Our teachers want us to come to *(him or her / them)* for help.

7. Josie and I bought *(their / our)* tickets yesterday.

Next Step Write five sentences that include pronouns and antecedents. Exchange papers with a classmate and underline each pronoun. Then draw an arrow to its antecedent, just as you did in the sentences above.

Indefinite Pronouns

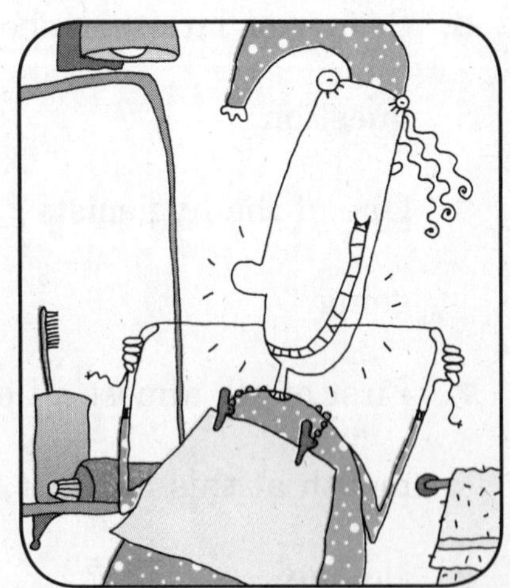

Indefinite pronouns do not have a specific antecedent. Some examples of indefinite pronouns are *any, either, none,* and *several.* See page 710 in *Write Source* for a complete list.

Be certain that these pronouns, when they are used as subjects, agree with their verbs. (See page 475 in *Write Source*, and see the examples below.)

Examples

Singular indefinite pronouns such as *each, either, one,* and *everybody* use a singular verb.

Everybody wants pearly white teeth.

The indefinite pronouns *all, any, most, none,* and *some* can be either singular or plural. How do you know which is which? Look at the prepositional phrase that follows the indefinite pronoun. If the noun in that phrase is singular, use a singular verb. If the noun is plural, use a plural verb.

Most of my life is pretty boring.
("Life" is singular, so the subject, "most," takes a singular verb.)

Most of my dental appointments, however, are not boring enough.
("Appointments" is plural, so the subject, "most," takes a plural verb.)

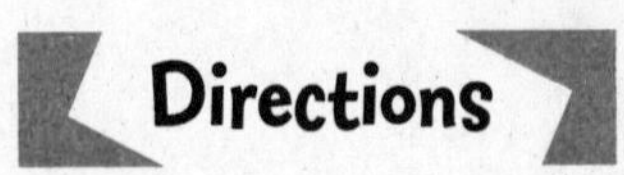

In the following sentences, underline the indefinite pronoun subjects once. Write the correct verb in parentheses on the blank provided. The first one has been done for you.

1. Everyone ___knows___ you're supposed to visit a dentist twice a year.
   (know, knows)

2. Nobody ___puts___ this in the same category as a visit to Disneyland.
   (put, puts)

3. Most of the dental offices nowadays ___are___ set up to calm the fears of nervous patients.
   (are, is)

4. Nothing ___bothers___ me too much about going to the dentist, except one thing.
   (bother, bothers)

5. Sooner or later, somebody in the office ___gets___ (get, gets) around to the crucial question.

6. One of the hygienists ___asks___ (ask, asks) cheerfully, "So, how's the flossing going?"

7. First of all, almost all of the dentist's hand ___is___ (are, is) usually in my mouth at this moment.

8. No one ___wants___ (want, wants) to talk at a time like this.

9. And none of the kids I know ___confess___ (confess, confesses) that they usually forget to floss.

10. The truth is that only some of my teeth ___are___ (are, is) easy to slip floss between.

11. ___Does___ (Do, Does) anyone have a perfect flossing record?

12. I'm always happy when someone ___hands___ (hand, hands) me my new toothbrush, and I can leave.

Next Step What's the best thing about visiting the dentist? What's your least favorite part? Write a paragraph that answers these questions. Use at least two indefinite pronouns and underline them when you are through.

Subject and Object Pronouns

Since pronouns substitute for nouns in a sentence, they are used in the same ways. For example, a *subject pronoun* is used as the subject in a sentence. A subject pronoun is also used after a form of the *be* verb (*is, are, was, were,* and so on). An object pronoun can be used as the object of a verb or the object of a preposition. The examples below plus the ones at 712.5 and 714.1 in *Write Source* illustrate these two uses.

Examples

I called Carla about our history assignment.
("I" is a subject pronoun.)

"This is she," Carla said when answering the phone.
("She" is also a subject pronoun used after a "be" verb.)

There are many similarities between you and me.
("You" and "me" are object pronouns.)

In each of the following sentences, write the correct pronoun in parentheses on the blank provided. Write "subject" on the line if the pronoun is a subject pronoun. Write "object" on the line if the pronoun is an object pronoun. The first one has been done for you.

subject **1.** Carla and ___I___ love to talk on the phone. *(I, me)*

object **2.** The telephone is the most wonderful part of technology for ___us___. *(we, us)*

subject **3.** When someone asks for you on the telephone, do you say,

subject "This is ___she___ *(she, her)*" or "This is ___he___ *(he, him)*"?

subject **4.** ___We___ *(We, Us)* both learned to recognize each other's voice on the phone.

object 5. On account of me, my mom rarely uses the phone.
(I, me)

subject 6. She said that the phone company should really be billing
(She, Her)

object me every month.
(I, me)

object 7. If my parents were interested, there are so many ways for them to improve our telephone setup.
(they, them)

object 8. Without you and me, our families would be so boring.
(I, me)

subject 9. Should you and I go swimming this weekend?
(I, me)

object 10. Please let me know about your grandmother.
(I, me)

subject 11. Mr. Smith is okay; he lets everyone talk at the end of class.
(he, him)

subject 12. Tomorrow's lunch is Katie's favorite; she just loves spaghetti casserole.
(she, her)

subject 13. The school cooks work hard; they just can't cook like my mom.
(they, them)

object 14. Who is going to the dance with them?
(they, them)

object 15. Don't believe what Josie said about Linda and me; I never
(I, me)

object said that I didn't like her.
(she, her)

Next Step Re-create part of a typical phone conversation with a friend. Circle two subject pronouns and two object pronouns in your writing. Share your results.

Possessive Pronouns

Possessive pronouns make your writing read more smoothly. Instead of repeating the same noun or pronoun, you can use the appropriate possessive pronouns, as in the examples below. (See 714.2 in *Write Source* for more information.)

Examples

Sheila wanted to use (Sheila's) cell phone.
(Sounds stilted.)

Sheila wanted to use her cell phone.
(Sounds much better.)

Sheila and I both needed to call (Sheila's and my) parents.
(Needs a possessive pronoun to stand for "Sheila and I.")

She and I both needed to call our parents.
(Correct)

On the blank before each sentence, write the correct possessive pronoun to replace the nouns or pronouns in parentheses. The first one has been done for you.

1. ___his___ Alexander Graham Bell tested *(Alexander Graham Bell's)* famous invention for the first time on March 10, 1876.

2. ___their___ Bell and Thomas Watson had *(Bell and Watson's)* first telephone communication after an accident involving Bell.

3. ___its___ The telephone is handy for all kinds of emergencies, and *(the telephone's)* first use was a sort of 911 call.

4. ___his___ Bell had just spilled battery acid on *(Bell's)* pants and called Watson on the telephone in the next room for help.

5. ___your___ Imagine what you might have said if you had just spilled acid on *(you)* clothes!

6. ___his___ "Watson, come here! I need you!" Bell said urgently into *(Bell's)* newfangled, untested device.

7. ___our___ We have to use *(we)* imaginations to envision what happened next.

8. ___their___ In the days and months that followed, Amos E. Dolbear, Elisha Gray, and other inventors claimed that *(Dolbear's, Gray's, and others')* telephone inventions had preceded Bell's.

9. ___his___ Over 600 claims were made against Alexander Graham Bell before *(Bell's)* claim of having been the first to invent the telephone was upheld by the U.S. Supreme Court.

10. ___my___ I appreciate hearing this story about Alexander Graham Bell, but one of *(I)* little questions has not been answered.

11. ___its___ Why did the Bell Telephone Company nickname itself "Ma Bell" if *(Bell Telephone Company's)* founder was actually "Pa" Bell?

12. ___their___ No matter which company provides it, people want *(people's)* telephone service to be fast, clear, and reasonably priced.

Next Step Create the dialogue that might have occurred between Bell and Watson after Bell's initial call for help. Underline the possessive pronouns you use. If necessary, refer to *Write Source* for help with punctuating dialogue.

Verbs 1

Both action and linking verbs are needed in writing. **Action verbs** add power and punch to a sentence. *Tumble, scream,* and *dream* are examples of action verbs. **Linking verbs** connect a subject to a noun or an adjective in the predicate. *Is* and *seem* are examples of linking verbs. Look at the example sentences below to see how each kind of verb works. (See 718.1–718.2 in *Write Source* for more examples of action and linking verbs.)

Examples

Many small children dream of becoming firefighters.
(The action verb "dream" tells what children do.)

Actually, firefighting is a difficult, dangerous job.
(The linking verb "is" connects—or links—the subject "firefighting" to "job.")

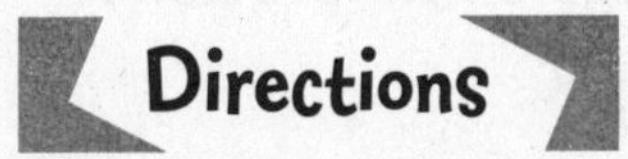

Underline the verbs with two lines in the following sentences. Label each verb with an "A" for action or an "L" for linking. (Two of the sentences have compound verbs.) The first sentence has been done for you.

1. Nearly everyone knows (A) about the great Chicago fire of 1871.
2. On the same night, an even more terrible fire roared (A) through Peshtigo, Wisconsin, 250 miles north.
3. At the time, Peshtigo seemed (L) safe, like any other busy logging town.
4. The summer and fall of 1871 were (L) unusually hot and dry throughout the area.
5. During the night of October 8, numerous small fires started (A) in the dry forests around Peshtigo.
6. Fire brigades worked (A) as hard and as fast as possible.
7. But suddenly the situation grew (L) far worse.

8. The sound of an enormous, raging forest fire reached the ears of the terrified residents of Peshtigo.

9. In the darkness and confusion, people panicked and ran in all directions.

10. Two different groups of people dashed toward the river from two directions and met on a small bridge.

11. The people felt confused and frightened.

12. The bridge collapsed.

13. Meanwhile, throughout the area, buildings exploded in the extreme heat.

14. Only people in the river survived.

15. Fifteen hundred lives were lost.

16. Three years later, the determined survivors rebuilt Peshtigo on its previous site.

17. The once forested landscape looks different now.

18. Today, dairy farms cover the countryside.

Next Step Write five sentences about fire prevention and safety in your home. Underline and label the verbs you use, "L" for *linking* and "A" for *action*. If you end up with all linking verbs, write at least two more sentences, this time using action verbs.

Verbs 2

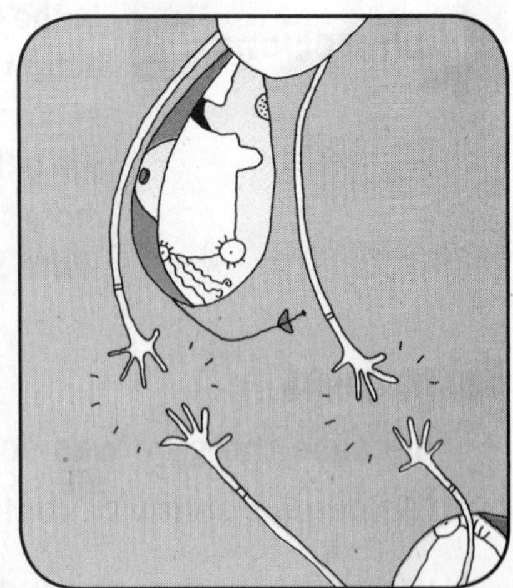

Swing, shimmy, and *shuffle* are lively, active words. They are fun to say and fun to use in your writing. These lively words have one important thing in common: they can all be used as **action verbs.** Not all verbs are action packed. Words like *is, are, was,* and *were* are called **linking verbs** because they "link" subjects to nouns or adjectives. Notice how these verbs work in the following examples. (See 718.1–718.2 in *Write Source* for more about these verbs.)

Examples

Joe expertly swung Debbie into the air at the last dance.
(The action verb "swung" describes what Joe did, and it brings the sentence to life.)

Joe and Debbie are good dancers.
("Are" is a linking verb that links the subject "Joe and Debbie" to "dancers.")

Underline the verb with two lines in each of the following sentences. Label each action verb with an "A" and each linking verb with an "L." The first two have been done for you.

1. The students entered the dance through the gym door.
2. The decorations were colorful streamers of crepe paper.
3. Our dance began right after school.
4. The theme of our dance was "Friends Forever."
5. Most of the students attended the dance.
6. Our disc jockey played a lot of oldies.
7. Most of us were very nervous at the beginning of the dance.
8. One of the chaperons arranged us in pairs to dance.
9. Larry and Jack hid from the "matchmaker."
10. Robert was the only nondancer in the group.

Directions

In the sentences below, underline each verb with two lines. Label each action verb with an "A" and each linking verb with an "L." The first sentence has been done for you. *Note:* Many of the sentences below are either compound or complex sentences, which means they contain more than one verb. See the examples below as well as the ones in *Write Source.*

Examples

Because the gym was so hot, we drank a lot of soda. (L: was; A: drank)

(A complex sentence contains two clauses.)

We had fun, though, and the disc jockey told great jokes! (A: had; A: told)

(A compound sentence contains two clauses.)

1. After the dance, we walked toward the beach. (A: walked)
2. We were hungry, so we stopped at a restaurant. (L: were; A: stopped)
3. Our waitress was friendly, and she asked us about the dance. (L: was; A: asked)
4. Larry told her that he was the best dancer there. (A: told; L: was)
5. We all laughed, because Larry is a terrible dancer. (A: laughed; L: is)
6. Down at the beach, the surf sounded louder than usual. (L: sounded)
7. According to Debbie, the TV news predicted a storm. (A: predicted)
8. Rick said that the storm was Larry's fault. (A: said; L: was)
9. "Your lousy dancing started a storm, Larry!" (A: started)
10. Everyone laughed at the joke, including Larry. (A: laughed)

Next Step Write three sentences about your own dancing experiences. (If you've never been to a dance, how about a birthday party with dancing?) Underline and label ("A" or "L") the verbs in your sentences. Share your results.

Helping Verbs

Auxiliary or **helping verbs** come before the main verbs; they help qualify main verbs—telling more exactly when and how the action of a sentence is taking place. Forms of *be, has,* and *do* are commonly used as helping verbs. (See 718.3 in *Write Source* for more information and a list of helping verbs.)

Examples

The dance was enjoyed by almost everyone.
("Was" is the helping verb; "enjoyed" is the main verb.)

The organizers could have sold at least 50 more tickets.
("Could" and "have" are helping verbs; "sold" is the main verb.)

In each of the following sentences, underline the verb with two lines. All but two sentences contain auxiliary or helping verbs.

1. However, the gymnasium at Fillmorton Recreation Center had become a disaster area.
2. Three students had been selected as the cleanup committee.
3. They were moving slowly through the debris on the gym floor.
4. They found Moe Epstein's baseball cap.
5. He may have lost it during his dance with Sasha Seabury.
6. Earlier, they had discovered Rachel Sveum's retainer under a heap of crepe-paper streamers.
7. She probably lost it during the swing contest.
8. That may have been the highlight of the dance.

Next Step Write three sentences on a subject of your choice. Use a form of the auxiliary verb "be" in one of your sentences and a form of the auxiliary verb "has" in another sentence.

Directions In the sentences below, underline each helping verb and circle each main verb. The first sentence has been done for you.

1. Everyone should stay and help with the cleanup.
2. But Rick reminded us that a storm was coming and we had planned to walk home.
3. Larry said he could call his dad.
4. "Maybe he can drive us home."
5. Larry called home, but no one answered.
6. Just then, we heard thunder.
7. A blast of wind cut through the gym and blew trash everywhere.
8. "Okay, I am not walking home in a storm," Debbie said.
9. We were wondering what to do when Larry yelled, "Dad!"
10. We all looked up and saw Larry's dad in the car right outside the gym door.

Next Step Write two or three sentences of conversation between Larry's dad and Larry and his friends on the way home. Use quotation marks correctly; underline the helping verbs and circle all main verbs.

Verb Tenses 1

We depend on a watch or clock for the time—except when we are reading or writing, that is. Then we must depend on the **tenses** of verbs to help us keep track of time. Verbs don't tell us if it's 1:30 in the morning or 3:05 in the afternoon. That's clock time. Verbs refer to time in a different way.

The **simple tenses** of verbs indicate whether an action takes place in the present, past, or future. The **perfect tenses** of verbs indicate special segments of time—such as when an action beginning in the past continues into the present. (See pages 720 and 724 in *Write Source* for more information and examples.)

For each of the verbs that follow, write sentences expressing the tenses, or "times," asked for. The first one has been done for you.

(Answers will vary.)

toss

I always toss bread crumbs to the ducks.
(present)

I tossed bread crumbs to the ducks.
(past)

I have tossed bread crumbs to the ducks.
(present perfect)

bake

I baked a cake for the picnic.
(past)

I will bake a cake for the picnic.
(future)

I had baked a cake for the picnic.
(past perfect)

list

I list ideas in my journal.

(present)

I listed ideas in my journal.

(past)

I had listed ideas in my journal.

(past perfect)

walk

I walk my dog in the park.

(present)

I will walk my dog in the park.

(future)

I have walked my dog in the park.

(present perfect)

Next Step Create another tense-writing frame for a verb of your own choosing in the space provided below. Exchange your work with a classmate and complete each other's frame.

____

(a verb of your choice)

____

(tense of your choice)

____

(tense of your choice)

____

(tense of your choice)

Verb Tenses 2

There are three simple tenses and three perfect tenses. By knowing how to use all six you will be able to tell exactly when the action of your sentences is taking place. (See pages 720 and 724 in *Write Source* for more detailed explanations and examples of verb tenses.)

Examples

Present Tense:
I cook.

Past Tense:
I cooked.

Future Tense:
I will cook.

Present Perfect:
I have cooked.

Past Perfect:
I had cooked.

Future Perfect:
I will have cooked.

Create sentences for each of the verbs below. Use the pronoun subject (*I, he, you,* and so on) and the tense, or "time," asked for. The first one has been done for you.

(Sentences will vary.)

1. walk *(we + future tense)*

   We will walk to the quick mart to buy a pizza.

2. order *(I + past tense)*

   I ordered . . .

3. hurry *(they + past perfect tense)*

   They had hurried . . .

4. help *(she + past tense)*

   She helped . . .

5. count *(I + present perfect tense)*

I have counted . . .

6. change *(we + future perfect tense)*

We will have changed . . .

7. try *(I + past perfect tense)*

I had tried . . .

8. ask *(she + future tense)*

She will ask . . .

9. plan *(he + present perfect tense)*

He has planned . . .

10. hope *(they + past tense)*

They hoped . . .

Next Step Write a simple story based on your sentence number 10 above. Then rewrite your past-tense story using one of the "perfect" tenses. Compare your results.

Irregular Verbs 1

The principal parts of most verbs are formed by adding *ed* to the main verb *(squish, squished, squished).* The principal parts of irregular verbs follow no set pattern *(bite, bit, bitten).*

Let's suppose you've been hired as an editor or a proofreader for your favorite magazine. You start reading through the stack of copy that's piled on your desk. Suddenly, you break out in a cold sweat. Every sentence seems to contain an **irregular verb.** Remembering the different forms of verbs like *burst, bring,* and *shake* drives you crazy.

What are you going to do?

Here's a suggestion: See page 722 in *Write Source* for a chart of irregular verbs. It will answer your questions about these troublesome words . . . and help you keep your job. You will also benefit from the following practice that addresses many of the words listed in the chart.

Study these irregular verbs. Read them quietly to yourself several times.

Present Tense	Past Tense	Past Participle
break	broke	broken
drive	drove	driven
eat	ate	eaten
fall	fell	fallen
give	gave	given
ride	rode	ridden

Note that these verbs have a certain rhythm that helps them stick in your mind. Now try some more.

Present Tense	Past Tense	Past Participle
catch	caught	caught
fly	flew	flown
rise	rose	risen
teach	taught	taught
wear	wore	worn
write	wrote	written

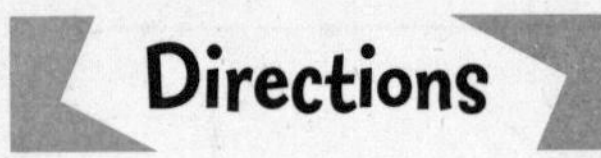

After carefully studying the chart of irregular verbs in *Write Source*, fill in the blank spaces below. (Have your book closed as you do your work. Refer to it only after completing your work.) Share your results with a classmate.

Present Tense	Past Tense	Past Participle
begin	began	begun
bring	brought	brought
burst	burst	burst
do	did	done
draw	drew	drawn
freeze	froze	frozen
go	went	gone
grow	grew	grown
lead	led	led
see	saw	seen
shake	shook	shaken
sing	sang (or) sung	sung
steal	stole	stolen
take	took	taken
throw	threw	thrown
weave	wove	woven

Next Step Write five sentences in which you purposely misuse some of the irregular verbs covered in this activity. (On the back of your paper, write each sentence correctly.) Submit your work for a class pool of "irregular" sentences that can be used for additional review work.

Irregular Verbs 2

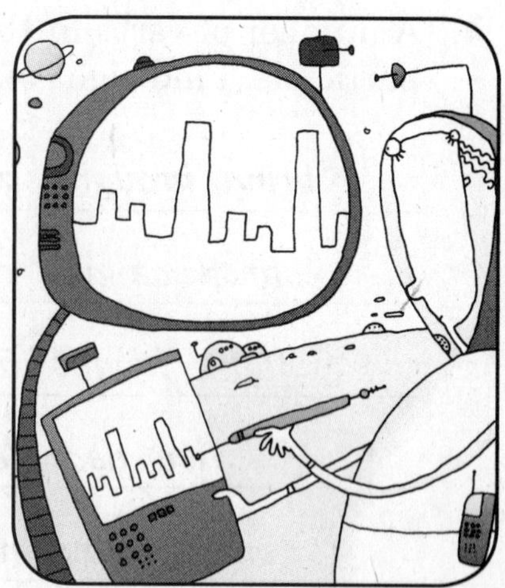

Regular verbs follow a simple pattern. You simply add *ed* to make the past tense and the past participle. Irregular verbs do not follow a simple pattern. Often, you use completely different spellings to make the past forms. Organizing irregular verbs into groups will help you remember them. (Turn to the chart on page 722 in *Write Source*.)

Directions **Using the chart of irregular verbs in *Write Source,* find the verbs that fit into each of the patterns below. After you complete your lists, read them over to yourself every now and then. Soon you will know these irregular verbs by heart.**

1. Look for the eight verbs that change only one vowel from present tense to past tense to the past participle. Write the three forms of each.

begin began begun | *sing sang sung*

drink drank drunk | *sink sank sunk*

ring rang rung | *spring sprang sprung*

shrink shrank shrunk | *swim swam swum*

2. Write two verbs whose principal parts (present tense, past tense, and past participle) are exactly the same.

burst burst burst | *set set set*

3. Find two verbs that have the same present-tense and past-participle forms. Only the past tense is different. Write the three forms of each.

come came come | *run ran run*

4. A number of verbs in the chart use the same form for the past and the past participle. Find eight of these verbs and write the three forms of each.

(Answers will vary.)

bring brought brought	lie lied lied
catch caught caught	make made made
fight fought fought	shine (polished) shined shined
flee fled fled	shine (light) shone shone
hang hung hung	sit sat sat
hide hid hid	sleep slept slept
lay laid laid	swing swung swung
lead led led	wring wrung wrung

5. Most of the remaining irregular verbs spell each of their three forms differently, with the past participle ending in an *n* or an *en*. List the three forms for 10 of this type. (There are many more!)

(Answers will vary.)

bite bit bitten	give gave given
blow blew blown	hide hid hidden
drive drove driven	ride rode ridden
eat ate eaten	speak spoke spoken
freeze froze frozen	take took taken

6. Finally, there are three verbs that don't fit any of the patterns you've just learned. Because they are used often, learn these, too.

am was been	go went gone
do did done	

Next Step Read through your lists of irregular verbs. Read them again . . . and again. With a partner, quiz each other on the irregular verbs you have learned.

Irregular Verb Review

Read each of the sentences below and decide which verb in parentheses is the correct choice. Write your choice on the blank in front of each sentence. The first one has been done for you. ***Remember:*** When helping verbs like "has," "have," or "had" are used, the past participle is required. (See page 722 in ***Write Source***.)

seen 1. Have you ever *(seen, saw)* Kansas City?

flown 2. I have *(flew, flown)* over the city a couple of times, but I have never actually visited it.

grew 3. Kansas City *(growed, grew)* up near the spot where the Missouri and Kansas Rivers meet.

brought 4. The possibility for river travel has often *(bringed, brought)* settlers to a place.

drawn 5. Some early settlers were *(drew, drawn)* to the area because of the trading and business opportunities.

came 6. That's how Kansas City *(came, come)* into existence.

risen 7. Four years later, the total population of the city had *(rose, risen)* to only a couple dozen people.

stolen 8. The town of Independence, 14 miles east of Kansas City, had *(stolen, stole)* all the attention in the area.

grown 9. Independence had *(grew, grown)* into a booming frontier city of 3,000 people.

drove 10. In Independence, pioneers outfitted their wagons and *(drove, drived)* west along the Santa Fe and Oregon Trails.

gave 11. Several events in the 1840s *(gaved, gave)* Kansas City the edge over Independence.

ran 12. The Missouri River shifted its course and *(ran, runned)* in a direction favorable to Kansas City.

brought 13. The California gold rush *(brought, brang)* 40,000 people through the city.

shrank **14.** The town of Independence *(shrinked, shrank)*, but Kansas City grew into twin cities, one in Missouri and one in the Kansas territory.

came **15.** Before the Civil War, slaves from Missouri *(come, came)* to Kansas, a free territory.

fought **16.** Bloody battles were *(fighted, fought)* during the Civil War in Kansas City.

known **17.** Today, Kansas City is *(known, knowed)*, among other things, for its cool jazz and great barbeque.

eaten **18.** If you haven't *(ate, eaten)* Kansas City barbeque, you haven't tasted real barbeque, according to the natives.

sung **19.** Jazz is played and *(sung, sang)* at many clubs across the city.

Transitive and Linking Verbs

Transitive verbs "transfer" their action to a direct object. The direct object completes the meaning of the sentence, as in the examples that follow. Linking verbs do not express action. **Linking verbs** link the subject of a sentence to a noun or an adjective, called the predicate noun or the predicate adjective. (For more information, see page 480 and 718.2, 728.2, and 730.1 and in *Write Source*.)

Examples

Transitive Verbs:

I raise ducks. I feed them.

("Raise" and "feed" are transitive verbs. Their action is transferred to "ducks" and "them," the direct objects. Direct objects are always nouns or pronouns.)

Linking Verbs:

Platypuses are swimmers.

("Are" is a linking verb that links the subject, "platypuses," to the predicate noun, "swimmers.")

The creature seemed frightened.

("Seemed" is a linking verb that links the subject, "creature," to the predicate adjective, "frightened.")

In the following sentences, underline each verb twice. Circle each direct object, predicate noun, or predicate adjective. (Don't forget that these can be compound. There may be two or three of them!) On the blank write "DO" for direct object, "PN" for predicate noun, or "PA" for predicate adjective. The first sentence has been done for you.

PN 1. The platypus is a native of Australia and Tasmania.

PN 2. Is a platypus a mammal or a bird?

DO 3. Scientists argued this matter for years.

DO 4. Like birds, platypuses lay eggs.

DO 5. Like mammals, platypuses nurse their young.

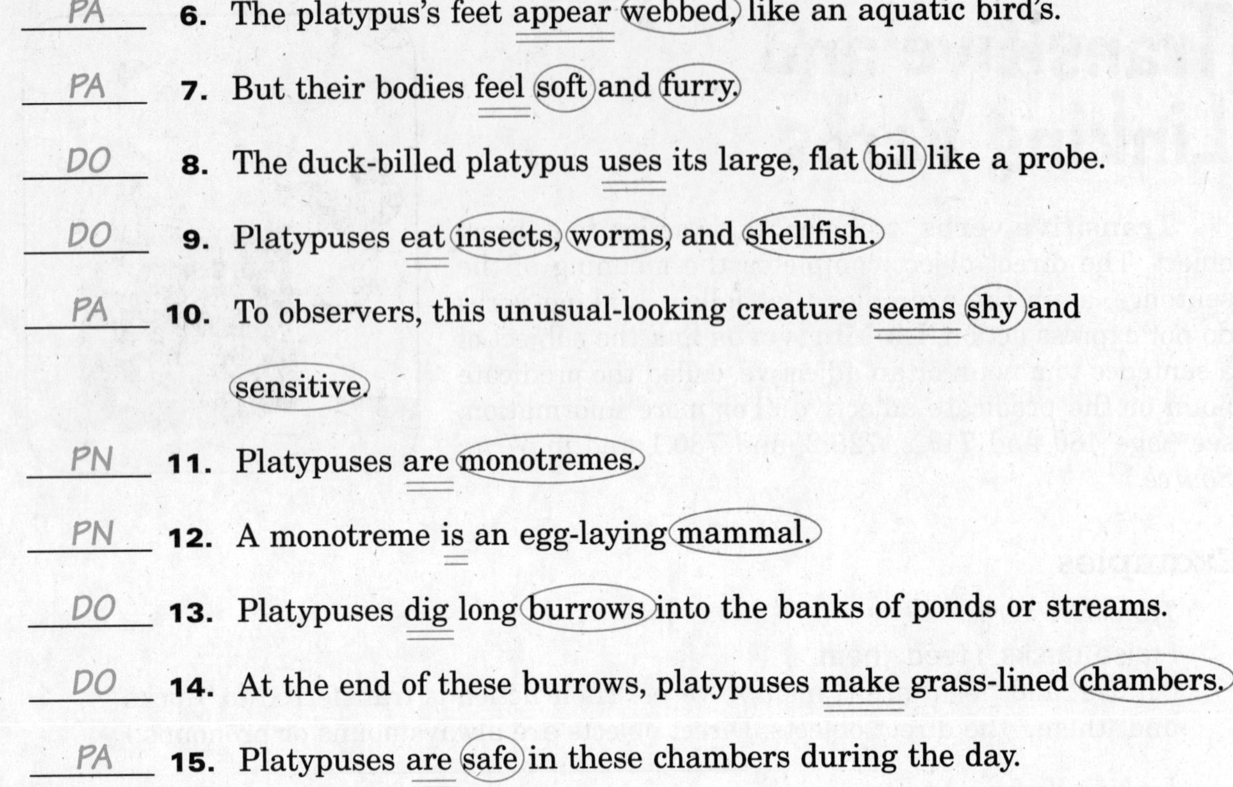

PA 6. The platypus's feet appear webbed, like an aquatic bird's.

PA 7. But their bodies feel soft and furry.

DO 8. The duck-billed platypus uses its large, flat bill like a probe.

DO 9. Platypuses eat insects, worms, and shellfish.

PA 10. To observers, this unusual-looking creature seems shy and sensitive.

PN 11. Platypuses are monotremes.

PN 12. A monotreme is an egg-laying mammal.

DO 13. Platypuses dig long burrows into the banks of ponds or streams.

DO 14. At the end of these burrows, platypuses make grass-lined chambers.

PA 15. Platypuses are safe in these chambers during the day.

Next Step Describe an animal that you know about by answering these questions: What does the animal look like? Where is it found? What does it eat? Who are its natural enemies? What special abilities does it have? Write a paragraph containing the details you've gathered. Now go back and underline all your main verbs. Circle and label the direct objects, predicate nouns, and predicate adjectives in your sentences.

Adjectives

Your best writing starts with a good writing topic. You must have a good story to tell (or some interesting facts to present). Then you must tell your story well. Specific nouns and action-packed verbs can add a great deal to your writing. **Adjectives,** which modify nouns or pronouns, can also help you tell a good story. Study the examples below to see how adjectives work. (See pages 732 and 734 in *Write Source* for more information and examples.)

Examples

Steve participated in two school activities.
(The adjective "two" describes how many activities. The adjective "school" describes what kind of activities.)

Yesterday, Steve left his baseball on the bus.
(The possessive pronoun "his" describes which baseball.)

Underline the adjectives in the following sentences. The articles "a," "an," and "the" should not be considered adjectives in this activity. (The number of adjectives in each sentence is indicated in parentheses.) The first one has been done for you.

1. Steve played on the sixth-grade soccer team. *(2)*
2. He also played first cornet in the jazz band. *(2)*
3. Steve was excited about the upcoming weekend. *(2)*
4. On Friday night, his parents were going to let him pitch their umbrella tent in the backyard. *(4)*
5. He had invited Dave and Greg and three other friends from his crowd. *(3)*
6. That night, they ran an extension cord from the nearby house and watched movies on a VCR. *(3)*

7. Later, Dave said, "We should cook some hamburgers and potatoes on the charcoal grill." *(2)*

8. The six guys wrapped the potatoes with onions and butter in heavy-duty foil. *(2)*

9. The aluminum foil protected the food from the hot coals. *(2)*

10. After an hour, the hungry boys couldn't wait to eat the delicious meal. *(2)*

11. Later, Greg let out a loud yell when he accidentally burned his right hand on the steel grill. *(3)*

12. Two family members and a next-door neighbor came to see what had happened. *(3)*

13. For a whole week, Steve felt good about the weekend. *(2)*

14. Then Dave wore a screaming Hawaiian shirt to school, and suddenly the camping experience was history. *(3)*

Next Step Write an acrostic poem like the one below. To write an acrostic poem, use the letters of a word to begin each new line. Each line should say something about the word. Have the poem describe an idea or a feeling like *love, freedom,* or *shyness.*

Example:

Lifting my heart
Over my head is
Very hard to do,
Except when you're around.

Note: An acrostic poem is also called a "title-down" poem.

Special Kinds of Adjectives

All adjectives describe nouns or pronouns. A predicate adjective is an adjective that follows a linking verb and describes the subject of a sentence, as in the examples below. (For more information on how linking verbs and predicate adjectives work together, see 718.2 and 734.2 in *Write Source*.)

Examples

Bats feel soft to the touch.
("Soft" is a predicate adjective linked to the subject "bats" by the verb "feel.")

Bats are fascinating.
("Fascinating" is a predicate adjective linked to the subject "bats" by the verb "are.")

Underline each subject once and each linking verb twice in the following sentences. Circle each predicate adjective. The first two sentences have been done for you.

1. Do bats seem frightening or mysterious to you?
2. It is true that bats are scary to many people.
3. Bats are small, but they eat plenty of insects.
4. Most bats remain hidden in dark caves during the day.
5. Bats are nocturnal, which means they are active at night.
6. A bat's webbed wings and big ears look unusual to some people.
7. Many people remain afraid of bats out of ignorance.
8. A healthy respect is good because bats can be rabid.
9. But bats are valuable, too, for preying on mice, mosquitoes, and other pests.

10. Through widespread slaughter and environmental damage, some bat species became rare in the 1980s.

11. Scientists appear concerned that the disappearance of bats could be upsetting to the earth's ecology.

12. For one thing, bats are valuable because they pollinate plants as they feed.

13. Bats are also useful for spreading the seeds of fruits, trees, and flowers.

14. It is popular to care about whales, wolves, and spotted owls; but bats are worthy, too.

Next Step To find out more about bats and how you can help keep them off the endangered list, write a letter to Bat Conservation International, P.O. Box 162603, Austin, TX 78716.

Forms of Adjectives

The *positive* form of an adjective does not compare a noun to anything else (*old* house). The *comparative* form compares two nouns (*older* house). The *superlative* form compares three or more nouns (*oldest* house). Some adjectives have irregular forms (*good, better, best* and *bad, worse, worst*). Others add *more* in the comparative form and *most* in the superlative form. (For more information, see 734.4–734.5 in *Write Source*.)

Examples

Positive Forms:
California is a big state.
New York is a populous state.

Comparative Forms:
Texas is bigger than California.
Texas is more populous than Alaska.

Superlative Forms:
Alaska is the biggest state of all.
California is the most populous state of all.

In the following sentences, write the correct form of the adjective in the parentheses on the line provided. In the blank in front of each sentence, write "P" for positive, "C" for comparative, or "S" for superlative to indicate which form it is. The first sentence has been done for you.

1. __S__ What is the __most gigantic__ country in the world.
(gigantic, most gigantic)

2. __S__ Out of all of the countries, Russia is by far the __most massive__ with more than 6.5 million square
(more massive, most massive)
miles within its borders.

3. __C__ Canada is slightly __larger__ than the Unites States
(larger, more larger)
__C__ in size, but its population is much __smaller__.
(smaller, more smaller)

4. ___S___ China, of course, has the ___greatest___ number of
(greatest, most greatest)
people—1.2 billion—of all the countries in the world.

5. ___C___ By the year 2050, the United Nations predicts that India will have grown ___larger___ than China in population.
(larger, more larger)

6. ___S___ In that same year, the five ___most___ populous countries
(more, most)
in the world will be (1) India, (2) China, (3) Pakistan, (4) the United States, and (5) Nigeria.

7. ___S___ Did you notice that the three ___biggest___ countries in
(bigger, biggest)
terms of population are all in Asia?

8. ___S___ The ___smallest___ country in the world—1/5 of a
(smallest, most smallest)
square mile—is Vatican City, totally surrounded by Rome.

9. ___P___ Whether you live in a ___large___ country or in a
(large, more large)
___P___ or in a ___small___ one doesn't matter.
(small, more small)

10. ___P___ You are ___unique___ because no one is quite like you.
(unique, more unique)

Next Step Write four sentences that make comparisons. For example: "The Pacific Ocean is the largest ocean." Then exchange papers with a classmate and underline the adjectives. Label each other's sentences with a "P," an "S," or a "C" as you did above.

Colorful Adjectives 1

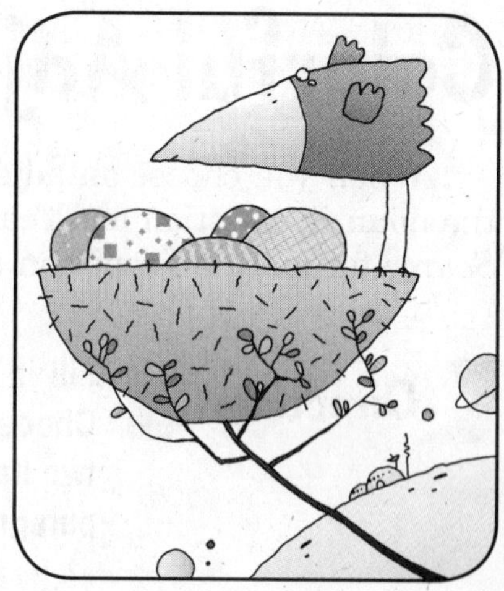

Whenever possible, use colorful adjectives to describe the nouns in your writing. At times, you'll need to dig deep to find just the right word to modify a certain noun. See the example below. (See pages 732 and 734 in *Write Source* for more information.)

The pencil bird is known for its uncommon eggs.

gigantic *patterned*

(The words "gigantic" and "patterned" are more colorful than "uncommon.")

Write three colorful adjectives that could be used instead of the overused adjective underlined in each sentence. (If you think you need help, use a thesaurus for this exercise.) *(Answers will vary.)*

1. Harvey Kennedy had a good idea for an invention—the shoelace. He earned more than $2,000,000 for his idea.

   fantastic *wonderful* *profitable*

2. Walter Hunt made a bad decision when he sold his safety-pin patent for $400. He never received any more money for his invention.

   poor *terrible* *unfortunate*

3. An inventor in Philadelphia had a nice idea when he combined a pencil with an eraser. He sold his patent for $100,000 in 1858.

   clever *brilliant* *inventive*

4. One man earned money in a different way. He allowed an advertising company to completely paint his van with ads.

   unique *strange* *unusual*

Next Step Decide which new adjective works best in each sentence. Circle your answer. Afterward share your work with a classmate.

Colorful Adjectives 2

When you choose an adjective to modify a certain noun, make sure it adds color to the noun in question and that it expresses the right feeling. (Turn to page 485 in *Write Source* for more information about the connotation of words.)

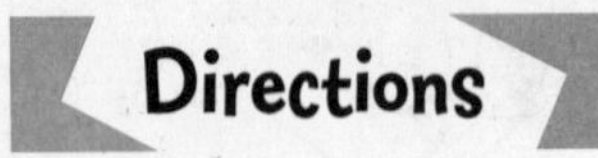

Fill in each blank in the paragraph with one of the two words listed. Choose the word that expresses the right meaning and feeling. (The two italicized words in the first sentence set the tone for the rest of the paragraph.)

Even in huge cities like New York, *friendly, gentle* pigeons feel right at home. In Central Park, I watch ____cooing____ *(cooing, awkward)* pigeons bobble around on patrol, searching for popcorn, scraps, and crumbs. On the ground, they look like ____miniature____ *(miniature, weird)* armies scavenging for bits of food as they go. Suddenly they turn and surround an ____old____ *(old, angry)* woman who sits on a park bench. She scatters crumbs from a bag of stale crackers. As the bag empties, the ____feathered____ *(silly, feathered)* soldiers march on in search of more handouts. Their ____gray____ *(gray, military)* uniforms act like camouflage as they disappear down the ____broad____ *(rough, broad)* sidewalk. These ____amusing____ *(amusing, strange)* birds are just as much a part of this ____wonderful____ *(wonderful, dirty)* city as cabs, subways, sidewalks, and skyscrapers.

Types of Adverbs

Words like *loudly, really, very,* and *never* are classified as adverbs. They are used to modify verbs, adjectives, or other adverbs. Adverbs fall into four different types or classes: adverbs of *time, place, manner,* and *degree.* (See page 736 in *Write Source* for more information.)

Example

Yesterday, Laura hurriedly flew over to inspect the dumpsite and almost fainted from the stench.

In the chart below, arrange the following list of adverbs according to the four different types. There are five adverbs per category. (Four have already been "charted" for you.)

yesterday **really** **lazily** **there** **soon**
over **carefully** **daily** **nervously** **scarcely**
hurriedly **forward** **here** **very** **everywhere**
almost **tomorrow** **hardly** **before** **brilliantly**

Time (answers *when*)	**Place** (answers *where*)	**Manner** (answers *how*)	**Degree** (answers *to what extent*)
yesterday	***over***	***hurriedly***	***almost***
tomorrow	*forward*	*carefully*	*really*
daily	*here*	*lazily*	*hardly*
before	*there*	*nervously*	*very*
soon	*everywhere*	*brilliantly*	*scarcely*

Next Step As a special challenge, add at least one more adverb to each of the four categories above.

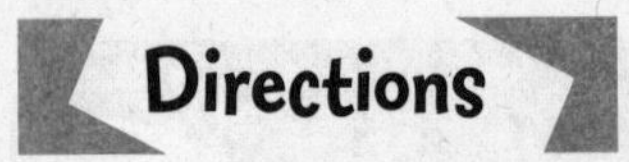

Write one sentence using an example of each type of adverb listed below. (Use the adverbs you charted on the previous page in your sentences.) *(Answers will vary.)*

adverb of time *Yesterday I slept for 13 hours straight.*

adverb of place *Your sneakers are here.*

adverb of manner *He read the poem brilliantly.*

adverb of degree *I could hardly believe my ears.*

Special Challenge: Really lay it on thick by using three or more of the adverbs from the chart in one sentence. (Write your sentence in the space below.)

I try daily to do my homework very carefully.

Next Step Use adverbs in a fun way by creating at least one "Tom Swifty." Two examples follow:

> **"Look at that punctured tire," my dad said <u>flatly</u>.**
> **"Stay down," the sergeant whispered <u>lowly</u>.**

In both examples, the underlined adverbs turn the statements into Tom Swifties.

Forms of Adverbs

Adverbs also have positive, comparative, and superlative forms. As with adjectives, some adverbs use *more* or *most* to form comparative and superlative forms. Other adverbs (such as *well, better, best*) are irregular and do not follow the normal pattern. (Refer to 738.2–738.5 in *Write Source* for more information.)

Examples

Positive Forms:

Joel runs fast.
Carlos reads rapidly.

Comparative Forms:

Joel runs faster than Carlos.
Carlos reads more rapidly than Joel.

Superlative Forms:

Ernesto runs the fastest of all.
Juan reads the most rapidly in our class.

In the following sentences, write the correct adverb form from the two in parentheses on the line provided. Write "P" for positive, "C" for comparative, or "S" for superlative on the line before each sentence. The first one has been done for you.

1. __P__ The first rules for soccer were published in London in 1863; but since then, the popularity of the sport has spread __rapidly__ across the globe.
(rapidly, more rapidly)

2. __P__ You must have good legs and lots of energy if you want to play soccer __well__.
(more well, well)

3. __C__ Soccer is played __less often__ than basketball in the
(less often, least often)
United States.

4. P Around the world, 100 million people of all ages and ability levels play soccer enthusiastically.
(enthusiastically, more enthusiastically)

5. P Over the years, soccer has steadily become more popular.
(steadily, most steadily)

6. C Soccer's popularity among women is growing more rapidly than field hockey's popularity.
(rapider, more rapidly)

Directions **Fill in an appropriate adverb in each sentence below.** *(Answers will vary.)*

1. On good days, I can run fast.
2. In the last game, I played badly.
3. Of all the sports, I love soccer best.
4. I would rather go to practice on Saturday morning than sleep late.
5. I practice better than my teammates do.
6. Lately, my team has been losing.
7. I need to work more carefully on my kicking.
8. Kicking the ball quickly past the goalie is hard.

Next Step Think of three sports that you enjoy watching or playing. Think of facts you know and your feelings about each sport. Write a paragraph comparing these three sports. Use at least one positive, one comparative, and one superlative form of an adverb in your writing.

Prepositional Phrases

A preposition is like a train engine. It has to pull something before it is useful. A preposition pulls adjectives, adverbs, and noun or pronoun objects. A prepositional train (actually a *prepositional phrase*) is a preposition and all of the related words it pulls.

Examples

into — the — bedroom
preposition adjective noun object

under — the — incredibly — messy — bed
preposition adjective adverb adjective noun object

in — one — determined — leap
preposition adjective adjective noun object

over — it
preposition pronoun object

Note: The words *a, an,* and *the* are special types of adjectives called articles.

Make three prepositional trains of your own, using the list of prepositions in *Write Source* as a general guide. (See page 742 in *Write Source* for this information.)

(Answers will vary.)

throughout — the — night
preposition adjective noun object

down on — the — farm
preposition adjective noun object

under — the — table
preposition adjective noun object

Next Step As a special challenge, label the parts in your trains as shown in the examples above.

Directions **In the space below, use each of your prepositional trains in a sentence.** *(Answers will vary.)*

1. *I watched for the meteor shower throughout the night.*

2. *We went strawberry picking down on the farm.*

3. *My dog begs for food under the table.*

Directions **On the lines below, keep writing the same sentence, but change the preposition each time—as many times as possible.**

Freezer Breezer swam alongside of the whales.
(Some prepositions like *alongside of* consist of two words.)

The scuba diver swam under the whales.

The scuba diver swam over the whales.

The scuba diver swam beneath the whales.

The scuba diver swam between the whales.

The scuba diver swam around the whales.

Next Step Exchange your work with a classmate and see who was able to use the most prepositions.

Interjections

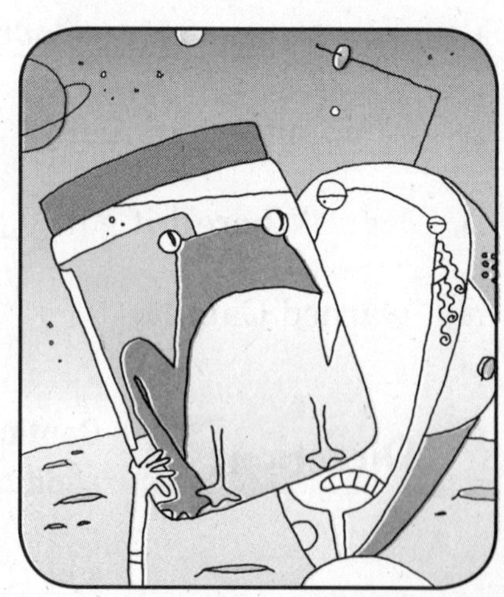

An **interjection** is a word that expresses strong emotion or surprise. Interjections are especially useful when you are writing dialogue for a play or a story. Either an exclamation point or a comma is used to separate an interjection from the rest of the sentence. (Turn to page 746 in *Write Source* for more about interjections.) Note the interjections (highlighted) in the following examples.

Examples

Yech! Why do we have to study pickled frogs?

Hmm, I think I'll leave mine in the jar.

Underline each interjection in the story that follows. Supply an interjection when a space is provided. The first one has been done for you.

(Answers will vary.)

"Wow, Camille! Look at that!" screamed Jana.

"Good grief, Jana, what happened?"

"___Well___! You're not going to believe this, but my pickled frog just moved inside the jar."

"Oh, sure, and my frog has wings," laughed Camille.

"Hey, I'm telling the truth. Look for yourself if you don't believe me."

"Okay, but this better not be a trick. You know how much I like surprises," warned Camille.

"No way, this is the real thing. I'll take the lid off the jar so you can get a closer look."

"___Yikes___!" screamed Camille as the frog jumped out of the jar, into her lap, and onto the floor.

"Yech! Just moving was bad enough; jumping is too freaky," shuddered Jana.

"Where'd it go? Oh no, we'd better go find it!" warned Camille.

Directions Continue the conversation on the lines below. Include at least three additional interjections. (Use your own paper if you need more space.)

(Answers will vary.)

Next Step Exchange conversations with a classmate. Note how your partner used interjections in his or her work.

Coordinating Conjunctions

Coordinating conjunctions are needed to connect words, phrases, and clauses in sentences. The parts being connected must be equal or of the same type. (For more information, see 744.1 in *Write Source*.)

Examples

Do you like to draw or paint?
(The words "draw" and "paint" are connected by the conjunction "or.")

I like to draw, but painting is difficult for me.
(The two clauses of the compound sentence are connected by the conjunction "but.")

Circle the coordinating conjunction in each of the following sentences. Underline the parts that the conjunction connects. The first two sentences have been done for you.

1. Because artists created lifelike paintings long before there were cameras, we can see many of the people, places, and events of the past.
2. Some artists paint realistic portraits of people, still lifes, and landscapes.
3. Three famous landscape artists are Jan Vermeer from Holland, Katsushika Hokusai from Japan, and Georgia O'Keeffe from the United States.
4. Art can express a feeling of happiness, joy, sadness, fear, or rage.
5. The oldest paintings in the world are more than 30,000 years old, yet they were unknown to us until recently.

6. We did not know of the paintings' existence, (for) they were hidden in caves in southwestern France.

7. We do not know the names of the artists who painted these cave walls, (but) we do know they were fine artists.

8. They made their paints out of colored earth (and) animal fat (or) charcoal.

9. Of course, we cannot know this for sure, (but) the people who lived long ago probably believed the cave paintings had magical powers.

10. There is something magical about art, (but) it requires hard work to develop artistic skill.

11. Street artists often attract a crowd, (for) everyone wants to see how the "magic" is done.

Next Step Write three additional sentences about a street artist or musician you've seen or heard. Use at least one coordinating conjunction in each sentence.

Subordinating Conjunctions

A reader must make many connections in a piece of writing, moving from one idea to the next. To make sure that readers are able to follow ideas smoothly and easily, writers often use **subordinating conjunctions.** See the examples below. (Also see 746.1 in *Write Source* for more information about conjunctions.)

Examples

Shorter Sentences:
Tasha loves creamed asparagus on toast. Her older brother Michael doesn't even like to look at it.

Combined Sentence:
Tasha loves creamed asparagus on toast, although her older brother Michael doesn't even like to look at it.
(The sentences are connected with the subordinating conjunction "although.")

Shorter Sentences:
My little sister's swimming pool was "bleeding." I applied a big bandage.

Combined Sentence:
Because my little sister's swimming pool was "bleeding," I applied a big bandage.
(The sentences are connected with the subordinating conjunction "because.")

Review the list of conjunctions in *Write Source*. Then practice using conjunctions by combining the following pairs of brief sentences into longer, smoother-reading ones. Try to use a different connecting word in each of your new sentences. *(Answers will vary.)*

1. Lucille tried on many bathing suits. Not one of them fit her right.

   Even though Lucille tried on many bathing suits, not one of them fit her right.

2. Father thought he had hooked a huge fish. Fred got the big net.

Because Father thought he had hooked a huge fish, Fred got the big net.

3. Finish your homework. You can go to the park.

After you finish your homework, you can go to the park.

4. My dog Oscar's belly almost drags on the ground. I can't bear to put him on a diet.

Although my dog Oscar's belly almost drags on the ground, I can't bear to put him on a diet.

5. Turn left at this corner. You'll end up in a deep pit.

If you turn left at this corner, you'll end up in a deep pit.

Next Step Trade papers with a classmate and see what conjunctions your partner used in his or her sentences. Then write three sentences using the following **correlative conjunctions:** *either, or; neither, nor;* and *both, and.*

Conjunctions Review

There are many kinds of conjunctions besides *and, but, or, nor, for, so,* and *yet.* All of them help connect the parts of sentences so that the sentences read smoothly and make sense. (Review page 496 in *Write Source* and look at the list of conjunctions on page 744.)

Read the following paragraph of short, choppy sentences. Rewrite the paragraph, using conjunctions so that it flows like "silk." You may drop words or change verb tenses if you need to.

The Silk Road was a trade route. It connected China to Rome. People began using this route about 100 B.C.E. Silk from China was carried on it. Gold from Rome was carried on it. Silver from Rome was carried on it. Caravans met on the road. They traded goods. They traded ideas. The Roman Empire fell apart around 500 C.E. The Silk Road wasn't used much after that time. It had lasted 600 years.

Next Step In ancient times, people had the Silk Road. Today, we have the Information Highway. How will people communicate and trade a hundred years from now? Write your predictions in a paragraph. Use conjunctions.

Parts of Speech Review 1

Directions Each "coin" contains a list of words representing one of the eight parts of speech. Identify the part of speech for each list of words on the blank space provided within each coin. Work on this activity with a partner if your teacher allows it. (Turn to page 748 in *Write Source*.)

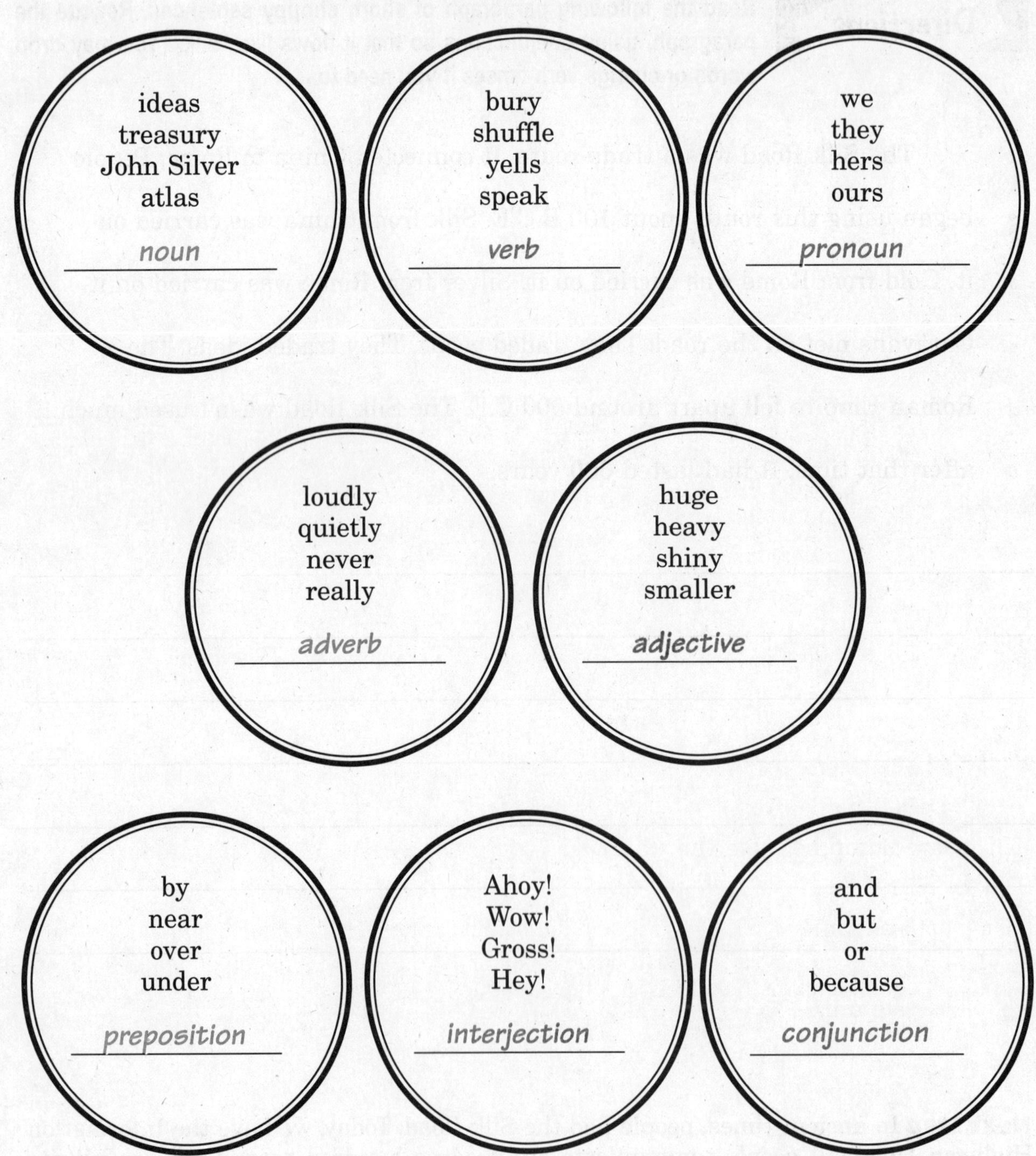

Parts of Speech Review 2

Directions Identify the part of speech for each underlined word below. Check the boxes below to keep track of how more many you need to find. The first sentence has been done for you. (Turn to page 748 in *Write Source*.)

nouns	☐ ☐ ☐ ☐ ☐	adjectives	☐ ☐ ☐ ☐ ☐
verbs	☐ ☐ ☐ ☐ ☐	prepositions	☐ ☐ ☐ ☐ ☐
pronouns	☐ ☐ ☐ ☐ ☐	conjunctions	☐ ☐ ☐ ☐ ☐
adverbs	☐ ☐ ☐ ☐ ☐	interjections	☐ ☐

Last Saturday, the public pool finally *(adverb)* opened for *(preposition)* the summer. My friend Sharla and I *(pronoun)* had been waiting for what seemed like months. Come to think of it, it had been two *(adjective)* months. Anyway, we were *(verb)* there bright and early *(adverb)*, even though it was only about *(preposition)* 65 degrees outside. Sharla was wearing a plain blue *(adjective)* swimsuit *(noun)*. I had eagerly *(adverb)* bought a swimsuit, too, but mine *(pronoun)* was made from a silvery green, striped *(adjective)* material.

Within *(preposition)* an hour, the whole neighborhood showed up. Well *(interjection)*, there might have been one or *(conjunction)* two kids missing. Sharla looked *(verb)* like a big, blue-lipped *(adjective)* goose bump because *(conjunction)* the water was so *(adverb)* cold. We had *(verb)* a great time, though. Carl and Burton, two boys from *(preposition)* the eighth grade, did belly flops off the low-dive until they *(pronoun)* were covered with red blotches *(noun)*. Sharla and I had an underwater swimming <u>contest</u> *noun*, and <u>some</u> *pronoun* of our friends <u>practiced</u> *verb* <u>synchronized</u> *adjective* swimming.

There was only one bad moment. <u>As</u> *conjunction* we were walking home, a <u>storm</u> *noun* poured rain on us. Suddenly, <u>lightning</u> *noun* struck a light pole <u>and</u> *conjunction* shattered the bulb. "<u>Wow</u> *interjection*! Did you see that?" I screamed. We hid <u>under</u> *preposition* a bridge until the rain stopped. Then <u>we</u> *pronoun* walked home quickly. <u>Though</u> *conjunction* we were cold and wet, we <u>had</u> *verb* a <u>really</u> *adverb* great first day at the pool.

Parts of Speech Review 3

Directions **Identify the part of speech for each underlined word below. Check the boxes to keep track of how many more you need to find.** **(Turn to page 748 in *Write Source*.)**

nouns	☐☐☐☐☐☐☐☐☐☐
verbs	☐☐☐☐☐☐☐☐☐☐
adjectives	☐☐☐☐☐☐☐☐☐☐
interjection	☐
pronouns	☐☐☐☐☐
adverbs	☐☐☐☐☐
conjunctions	☐☐☐☐☐
prepositions	☐☐☐☐☐

Most state names tell (*verb*) you something about (*preposition*) the state's beginnings, so (*conjunction*) it's not surprising (*adjective*) that many states have Native American (*adjective*) names. After all, who (*pronoun*) was here first? Chances are fifty-fifty, in fact, that your (*pronoun*) state name was borrowed (*verb*) from a word in the language of (*preposition*) the Native Americans who lived there (*adverb*) first. Alabama, Kansas, and (*conjunction*) Tennessee are three examples of states named after words in (*preposition*) the Creek, Lakota, and Cherokee (*adjective*) languages.

If your state does not (*adverb*) have a Native American name, chances (*noun*) are fairly (*adverb*) good that it has (*verb*) an English name (*noun*), especially if it was one of the original (*adjective*) colonies. Eight of the thirteen (*adjective*) colonies were named (*verb*) after English royalty or (*conjunction*) places in England (*noun*). Virginia was (*verb*) named after Queen Elizabeth (*noun*) of England, who was called (*verb*) the "Virgin Queen" because she never (*adverb*) married. Georgia (*noun*) was named after King George II. (His (*pronoun*) son was the ruler (*noun*) the colonists fought (*verb*)

preposition verb
against during the Revolutionary War.) New Hampshire got its name from a
preposition noun
homesick English settler from Hampshire, England, and the same goes for
noun
New Jersey, named after the English island of Jersey.

adjective pronoun adverb
About half a dozen states, including three of our most heavily
noun adjective
populated—Florida, Texas, and California—have Spanish names, while a
pronoun conjunction verb
few have French or Dutch names. That leaves Pennsylvania, which was
verb adjective adjective
named after its peace-loving founder, William Penn, and the state of
conjunction adjective
Washington; but I hope you don't need me to tell you who that state was
interjection noun
named after. Hey, he was our first president!

Next Step Use your classroom or library encyclopedias to learn about the early history of your state. Write a paragraph using the most interesting facts and details you find. Underscore any 10 words and label each according to its part of speech.